SUBTLE WORDS THAT SELL

How To Get Your Prospects To
Convince Themselves To Buy Without
Pushing, Pressuring, or Pitching.

Paul Ross

SUBTLE WORDS THAT SELL

How To Get Your Prospects To Convince Themselves To Buy Without Pushing, Pressuring, Or Pitching.

Copyright © Ghita Services Inc. 2019

All rights reserved. No part of this book may be reproduced, stored in a retrieval system, or transmitted in any form or by any means without the written permission of the publisher.

Printed in the United States of America.

DISCLAIMER AND/OR LEGAL NOTICES

While the publisher and authors have used their best efforts in preparing this book, they make no representations or warranties with respect to the accuracy or completeness of the contents of this book. The advice and strategies contained herein may not be suitable for your situation. You should consult a professional where appropriate. Neither the publisher nor the authors shall be liable for any loss of profit or any other commercial damages, including but not limited to special, incidental, consequential, or other damages. The purchaser or reader of this publication assumes responsibility for the use of these materials and information. Adherence to all applicable laws and regulations, both advertising and all other aspects of doing business in the United States or any other jurisdiction, is the sole responsibility of the purchaser or reader.

This book is intended to provide accurate information with regards to the subject matter covered. However, the Author and the Publisher accept no responsibility for inaccuracies or omissions, and the Author and Publisher specifically disclaim any liability, loss, or risk, whether personal, financial, or otherwise, that is incurred as a consequence, directly or indirectly, from the use and/or application of any of the contents of this book.

. . . .

Book Paul Ross
as your next great Speaker, Trainer, or Teacher.

Ross is available for:

- Keynotes
- Breakout presentations
- Speaking to groups and organizations
- Training of large or small teams
- Seminars and teaching

To contact Paul's team for inquires/booking, go to SpeakerPaulRoss.com.

Table of Contents

Acknowledgements	vii
Introduction	1
Part I Maximizing Your Mindset for Subtle Sales Success	13
Ch. 1 Build a Mindset That Truly Works	15
Ch. 2 The Power of "Ownership Language"	21
Ch. 3 Acceptance Confidence and Loving Uncertainty	27
Part II The Fundamental Principles Of Subtle Selling	33
Ch. 4 Foundations First: The Core Principles of Subtle Selling	35
Part III The Basic Building Blocks and Tools of Subtle Selling	45
Ch. 5 Commands and Suggestions	47
Ch. 6 Presuppositions	53
Ch. 7 Subtle Setup Phrases	61
Part IV Advanced Tools	65
Ch. 8 False Profession of Ignorance and Trance Phrases	67
Part V The Subtle Art Of Destroying Objections	73
Ch. 9 Subtle Power Words and Phrases to Easily Crush Objections	75
Ch. 10 Agreement Frames	81
Ch. 11 The Redefine Pattern	83
Part VI The Bonus Transcripts	89
Ch. 12 Subtle Words in Action: A Training Session With a Financial Services Professional	91
Ch. 13 Subtle Words for Super-Agents	113
Postscript	135

Acknowledgments

This book is dedicated to the following people:

To my parents, Irving and Sylvia. May their memories be a blessing.

To the giants upon whose shoulders I have stood:

Dr. Milton H. Erickson, father of modern hypnotherapy. And Richard Bandler and John Grinder, the creators of Neuro-Linguistic Programming.

To my nephews Ari, Gideon, Gabriel, and Eitan: my best friends, brothers, and surrogate sons.

To my mentor, champion, and friend, Greg S. Reid, who has been with me every step of the way.

To my friend, brother-from-another-mother, and operations manager Adam Hommey, MBA, without whom I simply would not be in business.

To my mentor, the late, great, Gary C. Halbert, the Prince of Print and perhaps the greatest copywriter who ever lived.

To my sister-from-a-different-mister, Sherri Olson-Hewitt, for seeing me through dark times and light times, good times and bad.

To my siblings, Alan, Marion, Anita and Steve. Thanks for teaching me the art of dinner table argument and debate.

To Dave Bozek for bringing order to the chaos.

To Kelly Roach, the world's best business coach. Thank you for all the hand-holding, cheering and butt kicking. You are the best.

To my best friend and favorite Swedish person in the world, Malin Fagerlund. Jag älskar dig min kära vän!

To my students who have inspired me for three decades.

And finally, to all those who are as madly, passionately in love with language and its power to turn stumbling blocks into stepping stones, pain into passion, and sorrow into solutions.

"And now," said Aslan presently, "to business. I feel I am going to roar. You had better put your fingers in your ears."

—C. S. Lewis

Introduction

My name is Paul Ross, and people call me the Wizard of Subtle Words That Sell®.

I want to make an outrageous, bold and audacious claim right from the get-go. Here it is:

If you use just 1/10th of the principles and tools I will teach you in this book, you will likely see at least a 15–20% improvement in your sales, conversions, and closings, with less work and far more fun.

Yes; when you know how to be subtle with your words, selling can be one of the most fun activities you can do and make lots of money at the same time—*especially when you know how to get your prospects to convince themselves to buy!*

Now, here comes a far more outrageous claim: If you use all of the principles, and tools, if you practice and apply them diligently, then you might very well enjoy a 50–200% improvement.

How can I make such a bold, even seemingly absurd statement?

Well, first and foremost, thousands of my students and clients from around the world have used what I'm about to teach you to get results just like what I've claimed.

Even more intriguingly, they have done it without having to fall back on tired old scripts, "yes ladders," tag questions (they bore you, do they not?) and worst of all, high-pressure tactics that just don't work.

But besides that, as you find yourself more and more drawn in to this book, you'll quickly realize that the principles you will be learning also make profound sense.

In fact, you may be surprised to find that it is almost as if your new understandings were filling in blanks that you never quite even knew were there.

As one of my students put it, "It was like everyone was saying the world was flat, but you were Columbus and helped me sail off the edge of my old map right into a New World."

I'm harping on this a bit because I want you to get full value from reading this book and using your learnings to your full potential.

So please go through the principles and concepts sections of this book before you proceed to the practical tools.

Now, please don't get me wrong. You certainly could skip to the tools section of this book and begin applying the subtle language patterns through pure memorization but with no understanding.

But, generally speaking, memorization does not lead to action. It leads to the illusion of progress, rather than a commitment to practice or the acquiring of actual real-world skill and wisdom.

Case in point: do you remember when you were in high school or university and you had to cram for an exam? Did it give you any real understanding of the subject matter?

Of course not.

Could you, if I asked, pass the same exam if I plopped it down in front of your face?

Dollars to donuts, you couldn't.

You fell victim to what I call "educational bulimia." You swallowed down the "knowledge" only to barf it all up on the test.

So, speaking to you as someone who is committed to massive success and true learning, and at the risk of repeating myself *please get the understandings before you apply the tools.*

I Love Selling, And You Will Too

As a kid, I grew up in a fairly lower middle-class home.

Now, get me right here: my father worked hard to put food on the table for 6 kids, plus my mother. In fact, he worked three jobs and busted his butt, and we always had money for books.

But if I wanted anything extra, I had to earn it for myself.

I got my first shot when it was during the third grade when it came time to sell chocolate bars to raise money for our elementary school.

You see, the kid who sold the most would get a whopping $10 cash prize (this was back in the early 1960s and $10 went a long way in those days) plus an award certificate.

Memorization leads to the illusion of progress, not to action or a commitment to practice.

Now, I was raised to be a contrary thinker. As my Mom said to me when I was around six, "Paul, whenever you are competing with people in anything that needs you to use your brains, look at what they are doing and do the opposite."

So that's what I did.

Before we were given our consignment of the over-priced bars, the teacher told us, "Just hold up the bar, smile and ask them if they'd like to help raise money for the school by buying some candy."

Thinking it through from the perspective of the potential buyer, I realized at that tender age that they were probably going to get bombarded by cute kids saying the same thing.

Plus, I instinctively knew that often times when you ask if someone would like to buy, it triggers an automatic "no."

So I took an opposite approach.

It went something like this.

Bell rings.

The door opens, an adult looks out and down.

Me: Hi. I'm Paul. I'm here to sell you something. (Holding up the bar). It tastes really good and you'll get to feel good while you eat it because it's helping out the school that makes this whole neighborhood a better place to live (dramatically spreading my arms and looking around me).

Now, I'm not kidding you—that's really what I said.

Did it work?

You bet.

In fact, let's start the learning and take it apart to see why It worked.

"Hi, I'm Paul. I'm here to sell you something."

This is an example of getting attention through interrupting the prospect's expectation.

Because lots of kids were going door to door and saying the same old thing, I created a bit of shock and got attention by saying something outrageous (and honest) right off the bat.

"It tastes really good and you'll get to feel good while you eat it."

The first part of the statement is true: of course, candy tastes good.

But then I used the subtle word "and" to link that obvious truth to the second part of the statement, which

- gets them to imagine eating it, thus presupposing that they will have bought it and
- tells them they are going to feel good about it.

Moving on:

"...because it's helping out the school that makes this whole neighborhood a better place to live."

Here I used the subtle word "because" to link in another, even more powerful benefit: that they will be helping out the school and making the entire neighborhood a better place.

This massaged their ego and made them feel important because they were making a contribution to the neighborhood.

A more abstract benefit than chewing on a gooey sugary confection to be sure, but a far more powerful one.

Read This Next Paragraph Very Carefully

You see, in my mind, I wasn't selling candy. I was selling a decision and good feelings about the decision. And perhaps even more importantly I was selling an opportunity to feel good about themselves.

From my point of view, I was doing them a favor and having fun rather than asking for something from them and feeling like a beggar.

(Imagine yourself and/or your team bringing that attitude and skill set into your selling as you find yourself wondering what that would do for your bottom line.)

It Gets Even Better

Subtle Words That Sell

So, do you think I was a clever kid?

Well, if so, you'll be really impressed by this next bit and how I once again used those two subtle words that sell, "and" and "because" to destroy the most common objection I got.

What was that objection?

"I'm sorry. I already bought one."

Now, what would most kids have done in that situation? What would you have done in that situation?

Most kids would have:

- Walked away dejected
- Begged or pleaded
- Talked about their desire to win the contest.

Once again, I broke the expectation of my soon-to-be-buyer by saying the following:

"Of course you did. And that's because you are a generous person who likes to make a difference. But I can only give you two because the guy down the block already told my mom he wants five."

Let's take this example apart.

"Of course you did…" I'm agreeing with him, so I'm taking any pressure off. There's not going to be an argument or a fight or an uncomfortable interaction with a poor dumb (ha ha) kid.

"And that's because you are a generous person who likes to make a difference."

Now I'm having the gumption to use those two fabulous subtle words to give him a name to live up to-being generous and wanting to make a difference. (I also happen to be using an advanced tool we'll use in Chapter 10: Agreement Frames.)

What's he going to say? "No, I'm a selfish, self-centered jerk."

Let's look at the next clever bit: "But I can only give you two…"

Now I was doing a lot of things here:

1. I'm defining the interaction as me "giving" instead of "selling" him something. I cleverly switched the frame of who was holding the value and who would be receiving it. (Frame setting is powerful. That <u>alone</u> could double your selling)

2. "I can only give you two" presupposes that he is going to want at least one. It's no longer a question of if he will buy, but if he will buy one or two.

And notice I did this without asking the stupid "either/or" false choice question that all the other kids were using (and that you've probably been using in your sales).

In this case, that stupid question would have been:

"Would you like one of those or two?"

I got to skip all of that by *implying* and *presupposing* that he was going to want at least one. Which also made it his own idea.

No pushing. No pressure. No pitching.

Pretty exciting, huh?

Moving on:

"Because the guy down the block told my mom he wants five."

Here I was incorporating scarcity and social proof, two of the major influencing factors in human decision making.

Needless to say, I won the competition by a landslide, breaking the $100 mark in two days and outsold the next closest three kids combined.

Selling Ethically: Persuasion vs. Manipulation

It's useful to look at selling as simply a subset of persuasion.

Now the tactics and tools in this book are going to give you tremendous power to influence and persuade your prospects on a very subtle level, and by that, I mean they will often bypass their own critical factor and get responses directly from their unconscious mind.

That being the case, it's important to address the ethical concerns about manipulation so let me draw the distinction, as I see it and practice it.

By manipulation, most people mean one or more of the following:

1. Hiding a harmful agenda. You say you are in love, but in reality, you just want to get close to someone to get your hands on their money.
2. Pressing hard on people's pain points: shame, fear, guilt, etc.
3. Concealing material facts. As an example, an automobile manufacturer failing to mention the exploding gas tank on their latest model.
4. Misrepresenting facts. Again, with the example of an automotive company, stating that the latest model gets 45 MPG, when in reality it is closer to 25 MPG.
5. Use of threats, force, or coercion.

By contrast, persuasion (and therefore selling) is all about:

1. Opening your prospect's mind to a decision that they didn't quite realize would benefit them.
2. Getting your prospect past their fixed, stuck, and autopilot perceptions, beliefs, unconscious sense of lack
3. Capturing and leading your prospect's emotions and imaginations.
4. Using your language to shape your prospect's decisions and drive their behavior.

Win/Win

All of this has to take place inside of a win/win frame.

The obvious reasons are that you want repeat business and referrals.

Remember, it's expensive to acquire a customer, but moreso to lose one.

And lose you will if your customer/client/prospect isn't happy because, after all, this is the "Yelp" generation.

It's been said that one angry customer outweighs ten satisfied customers, and if you check out the reviews on Yelp, you'll instantly and easily find yourself in agreement with this statement.

Finally, and on a more subtle level, taking on a "win-win" frame will subtly reinforce your belief that you are being of service, a powerful motivator that keeps you going through the often chaotic world of sales.

A Few More Notes Before We Dive In

The tools of subtle selling work most powerfully when used in combination, and try as I might, it's simply not possible to teach them in isolation.

So you'll find some examples may be repeated multiple times, but each time I'll reveal new tools within.

It's also crucial to understand that the subtle language patterns you are about to learn are meant to be spoken, not written.

So as you go through them, it will be very useful to speak them slowly, out loud, to get a feel for them.

Next, the tools I teach in this book are likely to be radically different than anything you've previously encountered.

On the positive side, this means you might eventually find yourself tossing out all of your old sales scripts, assumed closes, and other stale techniques as you grow increasingly comfortable using these new methods.

However, because they are radically different, on your first reading you may have some troubling responses arise such as, "This is just too far out there," "I can't see myself doing this," "This is confusing," or even "Paul is off his rocker."

When this happens (and it almost certainly will), I want to encourage you to instead get very curious and excited about your new learnings.

Why?

Simple.

It is the very ways of understanding and moving through the world that stand so far outside of what we are used to doing, that carry the potential to bring us results so far outside of what we are used to enjoying.

So get out there and practice. After a while, you'll have to bite your cheeks at how easy this stuff is and how powerfully it works.

Thanks in advance for the honor of letting me be your teacher and guide on this amazing journey into the world of Subtle Words That Sell.

Paul Ross

The Wizard of Subtle Words That Sell®
February, 2019
San Diego, California

I saw the angel in the marble and carved until I set him free.

— Michelangelo

Part I

Maximizing Your Mindset for Subtle Sales Success

Chapter 1
Build a Mindset That Truly Works

If I were to ask you how many books have been sold in the last 10 years on the topics of finding love, losing weight, and making tons of money, what would your guess be?

10 million?

20 million?

50 million?

Frankly, I don't know the exact answer, but I'm sure you can easily agree it certainly is in the millions and millions of copies.

Which raises the next question: why don't see millions and millions of skinny multi-millionaires with their ideal mates, happily in love?

It's clear that in between the inspiration/information and the implementation there is a big gap.

Put another way: there is something *profoundly, crucially incomplete* in what is being taught to get people actually and consistently moving forward in areas of life that have big emotional buttons like relationships, money, and personal appearance.

Here's what I think is going on.

The simplest answer is that all these subjects come with big emotional buttons that trigger old, self-defeating and fixed patterns of thinking, feeling, and acting.

If you have ever felt that, despite all the positive programming, vision boarding and affirmations, there is another aspect or part of you that has held you back, then you've seen this in action.

So if you really want to make all the positive stuff—the visualizing and writing down goals work—then you have to first take the steam out of the old stuff, have a good method for dealing with it when it comes up., and most crucially, avoid reinforcing and feeding it when you try to learn from your mistakes.

But be of good cheer, because I'm going to de-mystify that mechanism, show you all the moving parts that no one else has seen before, and then give you exact instructions to shut it down.

What Doesn't Work

It's been my experience over years of training that most salespeople are given motivational methods that are actually counter-productive to their success, and to be rude about it, sometimes plain stupid.

These myths get repeated sufficiently often and go completely unchallenged to the point where they are accepted as "truth" when, in reality, they are very ineffective for all but the most self-motivated people.

Here are the most common, inefficient and unworkable methods that you have probably been taught:

1. Get yourself into a peak state. This is the Tony Robbins school of pumping yourself up, jumping up and down and giving yourself super-pep talks, even doing fire walks.

   The problem with this approach is three-fold:
   a. Peak states can't be maintained. They are exhausting.
   b. If you are in a peak state, your enthusiasm is going to screw up your ability to pay exquisite attention to your prospect's actual responses.

c. Finally, your peak state is likely to fry your prospect's circuits. If they are cautious, bored, or just plain tired, you are going to lose them.

2. Push through the frustration and pain with pure dogged persistence.

To be sure, there is nothing wrong with persistence. We've all been rightly inspired by stories of brave people who struggle and carry on despite every hardship to reach their dreams.

But what happens when you are unknowingly persisting with something that doesn't work? What happens when you are pushing ahead with the very behaviors and ways of thinking that are keeping you trapped?

Here's a subtle and equally powerful point to consider: *if you are pushing through pain and frustration, then you are also unknowingly putting that emotional energy between you and your prospect.*

Just as importantly, pain and frustration are *a potent and volatile mix* and are very likely to *distort your perception and drive your behavior* right back into the very patterns that don't serve you.

In extreme cases, pain and frustration can so distort your perception, you might not even see that you are actually about to win.

When you are in the midst of this kind of emotional whirlwind, all the fortune-cookie advice in the world like, "One door closes, another opens" and "It's not how many times you fall but how many times you get up" isn't going to cut it.

The final piece of what doesn't work has to do with how you use your internal self-talk. Let's have a closer look at this.

Are you a chronic "Musterbater" and do you "should" on yourself?

Almost certainly, you are a "Musterbater."

No, I'm not talking about something that could get you arrested on the subway.

I'm talking about making self-statements like:

- I must make these follow up calls today.
- I must be more consistent.

- I must be more organized.
- I must not be so nervous.

Musterbating doesn't work because it produces no actual forward momentum or motivation. It merely produces the illusion or imitation of these things.

"Shoulding" On Yourself

Once again, we have a word that produces the illusion of forward momentum and motivation.

Statements like "I should make these calls today" or "I should go for the big money sales" don't give your mind anything to aim at, nor do they teach you any skills or help you understand the nature of your challenges any better.

They are forms of self-torture, thinly disguised as a motivational strategy, and self-torture never, ever works.

Always/Never Statements

I doubt that you are the kind of person who uses these statements, but if you've ever gone through a serious depression, then you probably have.

They take the form of, "I always screw it up with clients" or "I always blow it when it comes to the closing."

Or alternatively, they take the form of "I never reach my true potential."

The problem with these statements is that they are what I call, unbounded in time

There is no clear delineation as to whether they are statements about the past, observations about the present or commitments to the future.

In the world of cognitive behavioral therapy, these statements would be labeled "pervasive" because they are by implication, unchanging and unchangeable.

More Forms of Neuro-Linguistic Self Torture: Asking "Why" Questions

In my trainings, I often find that salespeople ask themselves questions like these:

- Why am I afraid to go after the big money clients?
- Why do I clam up when it comes time to make the close?
- Why can't I be more motivated?

I point out to them that when they ask "why" questions about what they've done in the past, they are actually and inadvertently getting their brains to dwell on their mistakes.

Now, here's a rule of the mind:

> "To Your Brain, There Is No Difference Between What You Dwell on and What You Are Programming It to Do."

Since the brain works on repetition and what is familiar, it's no mystery people who do this keep repeating their mistakes and less than useful behaviors.

It's not that they are "self-sabotagers" or have "low self-esteem."

They simply have a very ineffective learning strategy that is virtually guaranteeing they will keep repeating their mistakes.

The formula looks like this:

Ineffective behavior → Attempting to learn from it through dwelling on mistakes → Programming and reinforcing ineffective behaviors back in → Ineffective behavior.

This leads to a cycle of frustration, confusion, self-torture at worst, or very inconsistent, "three steps forward, two steps back" motivation and progress.

Throw in a steep learning curve and you've got a formula for making consistent, repeated and focus action toward your goals far more difficult than it has to be.

The tools in the next chapter will guarantee you never have any of these challenges again.

Chapter 2
The Power of "Ownership Language"

Here are three very powerful words to subtly influence your own unconscious mind and wipe out the habits of Musterbating and Shoulding on yourself.

1. Claim
2. Choose
3. My

Claim: when you go to the valet to drop off your car, they don't give you a "want" check.

No, they give you a "claim" check.

To claim implies ownership, authorship, and response-ability (yes, I deliberately spelled it that way).

So, notice the difference between saying:

"I must make these calls today" and "I claim my commitment to make these calls today."

Choose: How about this replacement?

"I choose to make *my* calls today."

Once again, to choose implies ownership, authorship, response-ability, and commitment. And it creates the forward momentum you need to create consistent action.

My: Notice the felt difference in your body when you say these two sentences out loud:

"I choose to do these calls today."

"I choose to do my calls today."

The word "these" puts an unconscious, subtle distance between you and your chosen action.

Putting the ownership word "my" into the statement solidifies and shows that you've willfully embraced the chosen action.

It works the same way with positive programming.

Note the felt, "in your body" difference between the following statements:

"I want confidence with prospects"

"I claim confidence with prospects.

"I claim my confidence with prospects."

"I claim my confidence with my prospects."

The difference is subtle. But subtle—as you will continue to see—is immensely powerful to influence yourself as well as others.

Use "How" Questions Instead of "Why"

Now we are getting to the nitty-gritty; the building blocks of what I call "learning confidence." That's simply both trust in, and efficiency at, learning from your experiences.

What we want to do here is, at all costs, avoid "why" questions and instead ask "how" questions such as:

"How could I have done better at this?"

"How can I find someone I can model or who will mentor me so I can learn what works?"

"How can I learn to recognize, first and foremost, what I did right and most effectively?"

With regard to recognizing what you did effectively and right, you might find it useful to employ these categories:

1. What you did right in your preparation. Period.
2. What you did right sequentially. Meaning, anything that occurs in a certain order, such as making the right introduction, guiding your prospect to reach the right conclusions, getting the order, etc.
3. What you did right throughout, such as maintaining the most effective state of mind, observing your prospect's responses, etc.

Three "Magic" Words to Annihilate "Always" and "Never" Statements

What if I were to tell you that there were three magic words that could forever end self-sabotaging and self-torturing "always" and "never" statements?

Well, here they are: "up until now."

It works like this.

When you catch yourself making a self-limiting statement like, "I always blow it when I go to close a big money client" or "I'm just not a great closer," you re-language it by saying something like:

"Up until now I didn't consistently close big money clients."

"Up until now I was not a great closer."

Putting the phrase "up until now" in front of the self-limiting statement is very, very powerful.

It acknowledges to the unconscious mind that there has indeed been a real problem.

We absolutely have to do this, or the unconscious mind will push back against any change we try to make.

Just as importantly, "up until now" *binds the perceived problem, limitation or block in time, placing it firmly in the past, opening up the neuro-circuitry for new possibilities, new skill sets and new outcomes.*

Incorporating Ownership Language

To add to the power of this, we can now incorporate ownership language into the new statement.

So, "I just can't close big money clients" becomes:

"Up until now, I couldn't close big money clients, and now I claim my mastery of my skills to easily close my big money clients."

Or:

"Up until now, it was the case that I didn't effectively close my prospects. And now I claim my ability to learn to effectively close my prospects, anytime, anywhere."

You might have caught that we are not suddenly making the leap to saying, "And now I recognize I am a fantastic, big money closer."

The problem with attempting to suddenly assign a winning identity to ourselves is that it doesn't set any direction for the unconscious mind to follow.

So when you re-language, as much as possible, make it about claiming skills/patterns of behavior/qualities of personality rather than about taking on a new identity.

The take-away is this: When we use our language effectively and with deliberation, we turn our stumbling blocks into stepping stones and spring boards to our success.

When we use our language effectively and with deliberation, we turn our stumbling blocks into stepping stones and spring boards to our success.

Chapter 3
Acceptance Confidence and Loving Uncertainty

In the previous chapter, I spoke about the importance of developing "learning confidence."

Digging a little deeper, I'd like to introduce the notion of what I call "acceptance" confidence.

A story to illustrate:

A few years ago, I was spending time with one of my VIP coaching clients.

One evening, we went to a local restaurant that had an outdoor patio where people mingled.

After a few hours (during which he actually succeeded starting some good conversations) we decided to leave.

As we were standing outside, waiting for our taxi, I noticed an attractive young woman standing fairly close by, waiting for her cab. (This was the days before Uber.)

I looked her way and very casually said, "Oh look. There's a lovely young lady waiting for her cab."

For some reason it went in the wrong way, and she got very, very angry.

She looked my way and screamed some very interesting suggestions about me doing some anatomically impossible things with myself.

My client grew visibly angry, his face reddening and his muscles tensed to go give her a piece of his mind.

I put my arm out, stopped him, and said the following:

"No, no, no. She can say whatever she wants. *We* decide where we come from."

Then looking right at her, I said, "She's someone's sister. She's someone's best friend. She's someone's daughter.

I paused a moment, took a breath and said, "Somewhere, she is deeply loved."

The change that came over her was dramatic.

She immediately burst into tears, ran over to me sobbing, threw her arms around me and held on to me.

"Oh my God," she said. "Thank you so much. That is the sweetest thing anyone has ever said to me. I'm so sorry for what I said. Men have been total pigs to me all night long."

Her cab pulled up, I bid her adieu and looked over at my astonished client, whose anger had also disappeared, in this case replaced with stunned disbelief.

Now, what made all this possible?

Instead of going into a reactive mode with this woman, I stayed neutral (remember what I said about the power of the neutral state of mind).

But far more importantly…

    I Gave Her <u>Radical Permission</u> to Have Her First Response to Me.

I didn't point the finger back. I did not hold any resentment toward her or think in any way that I was entitled to any politeness on her part.

I just let her be and extended my permission to be exactly as she was.

Please do your best to process this concept because it will not only help you in your sales career but your life in general.

99% of the people in the world are just not used to having someone hold this kind of space for them when they are being unpleasant, what to say being downright hostile and vulgar.

When you can remain neutral in the face of this and let them be just as they are, it serves a twofold purpose.

1. It interrupts their pattern of thinking and feeling, leaving them very open to being led. As I'll continue to point out through this book, pattern interrupts are extremely powerful ways to create windows of suggestibility and openness to seeing things your way.

2. On a deeply unconscious level, the other person will feel supported and "held" because you are not judging them.

Now, there is another principle at play. Because while I extended my radical acceptance to this young woman, I also didn't accept her first response as being her only response or her best response.

Why?

Because in virtually every context of life, I've taken this next principle to heart:

I Very Seldom Take a Person's First Response to Me as Written in Stone. It's Almost Always a Reflection of What They Are Thinking, Feeling, or Believing in That Moment and Almost Always Subject to Change.

Without having that attitude and frame around my communication as a foundation, I never would have been able to come up with the verbal response I did.

I would have made it about me and I would have seen her as a horrible person attacking me, not a human who was suffering.

Will your prospects treat you in as extreme a fashion as this woman did?

Almost certainly not. But if you are in sales, or leading a team of salespeople, you are going to have to deal with people who are often reactive in non-useful ways, and it's almost certainly going to happen quite often.

Say Goodbye to Your Need to Be Certain

It would be safe to say that the need to be certain is one of the fundamental drivers of human thought and action.

Over centuries, humans have fought endless wars over their need to be certain of their theologies, political systems, racial differences to name a few.

And if you don't think humans love certainty, just watch people argue about the merits of their favorite candidate during the Presidential election season.

It's actually quite entertaining to watch someone screen out any information that might undermine their candidate's perceived awesomeness and grow even more fixed, even fanatical in their support.

This happens on a personal level as well.

If you've ever had a friend who is madly in love, and you've tried to warn them about the negative qualities you see in their partner, you know what I am talking about.

Now it takes discipline and determination to let go of this need for certainty, but when you can do it, you are gaining a subtle and very powerful advantage of the 99.99% of the people on the planet who either don't grasp the concept or *would run like hell from the idea*, let alone the practice.

Note that I didn't say you shouldn't *want* or even *seek* a *degree of certainty*.

I simply said needing certainty is going to impede you.

Here's The Real Magic

When you can combine:

- radical acceptance of your prospect's first response to you
- interrupting their pattern, and
- not needing certainty about the outcome

… a doorway opens to a subtle, powerful and even magical connection that no outside observer would ever be able to figure out or explain.

Even better, *this connection continues <u>long after the initial transaction is over.</u>*

What does this translate to on a practical level?

> Constant and Consistent Repeat Business and/or Referrals, Often without You Even Having to Ask!!

Not a bad outcome for exercising some unusual concepts that are fairly easy to use and actually allow you to be much calmer, happier and much better leader, whether of prospects or your own team.

(Extra benefit: it works amazingly well in your personal relationships too.)

Give me a place upon which to stand and a lever large enough and I will move the world.
— Archimedes

Part II

The Fundamental Principles of Subtle Selling

Chapter 4
Foundations First
The Core Principles of Subtle Selling

Before we move on to the actual tools and practical examples, it's important to have you understand the conceptual foundation upon which they stand.

To return to the quote at the beginning of this Part of the book, the tools and techniques are the lever. The principles and axioms are the place upon which to stand.

With that in mind, let's get going.

> You are never actually selling your product or service. You are always selling decisions and good feelings about decisions.
> **Subtle Sales Principle No. 1**

Look: it's ok to be proud of, and passionate about your product or service.

But unless you've come up with cold fusion, wireless transmission of power or antigravity, it's very likely that you have or will have competition that offers something very similar.

And that means that essentially your product or service is a commodity like rice or potatoes.

Even if you are truly extremely better at what you do or your product is truly better by orders of magnitude, *you are still going to have to sell your prospect on the decision to buy and you are still going to have to get them to attach good feelings to that decision.*

So taking on this orientation is going to dramatically improve the results you get.

> Whatever you can get your prospect to imagine for themselves will be perceived by them as being their own thought and will not be resisted. Therefore, capture and lead your prospect's imagination and emotions before you present the facts, data and figures.
>
> **Subtle Sales Principle No. 2**

The basic (and admittedly grossly oversimplified) idea here is that you want to address and activate the right-brained, imaginative, and even childlike portion of your prospect's brain.

As much as we want to think we are all adults, making our most important decisions for carefully considered and well thought out reasons, it has been my observation that inside every adult, no matter how adult they may be walking through the world, is a 5-year-old child who wants to believe and be led.

If this is upsetting to you (personally I find it exciting), remember our discussion about ethics and the difference between manipulation and persuasion.

As far as I can see, there is nothing wrong with being crafty in the service of a process and proposition that serves your prospect as well as yourself.

Inside of every adult, no matter how adult they may be walking through the world, is a 5-year-old child who wants to believe and be led.

And given that at some point you will be presenting the data, your prospect will have every opportunity to critically evaluate what you present, albeit with their already having decided on the unconscious level they want to move forward.

> Nowadays your prospect no longer trusts their ability to make a good decision, and with good reason.
>
> **Subtle Sales Principle No. 3**

This principle is best illustrated with a story from my personal experience.

About a decade ago, my accountant called me around tax filing time and told me to make a contribution to my retirement account.

So I strolled into my trusty Washington Mutual branch, and asked to speak to the financial officer.

After introducing himself and listening politely to me, he asked me what level of risk I was seeking.

"Very conservative" I replied.

Handing me a slick brochure, he said, "I have just the thing. This insurance company is called AIG, and they have assets like you won't believe."

(If you remember AIG, I'm not joking. That's actually and exactly what he said.)

Now shortly thereafter, the real estate/mortgage business tanked and the "too big to fail" banks and insurance companies were bailed out to the tune of hundreds of billions of dollars, courtesy of you and I, the tax payers.

AIG was one of the worst cases. And Washington Mutual, once one of the most powerful financial institutions and trusted banks in the U.S., sank like a lead weight before being bought up by Chase for a dime on a dollar.

The point of this financial history lesson is that tens of millions of Americans got taken to the cleaners by the very institutions that had been the bedrock of their financial security and trust in the system.

The previously unquestionable ideas like, "you can take that to the bank" and "real estate never loses its value" suddenly were shattered and investment/financial decisions that used to make sense, no longer did.

That psychic trauma and mistrust of themselves is still lurking there in the background, especially in the financial services or real estate businesses.

So it's no longer enough to get the prospect to trust you.

You've got to subtly convince them that they can trust themselves when it comes to making the decision to part with their money.

> Your prospect no longer has the focus and concentration they need to make important decisions.
> **Subtle Sales Principle No. 4**

Oh for the days before cell phones, text messaging, the internet, Facebook, Twitter, LinkedIn, YouTube, Tinder (not that I know anything about that), Instagram, etc.

Today, our entire world seems to be orbiting around the dark star of cultural narcissism, distraction, overstimulation, and ADD/ADHD.

Here's a useful experiment if you doubt me on this one:

Simply go to a busy area at lunchtime and count the number of people who are walking around with their cell phones glued to their faces.

If you want to get totally real, just observe how many times you do this yourself throughout a typical day.

So even if your prospect wants to believe and is interested in your offer, don't count on their ability to stay focused long enough to pay attention.

You have to create these states of focus and create them within the first few minutes of your opening discussion.

Today our entire world seems to be orbiting around the dark star of cultural narcissism, distraction, overstimulation, and ADD/ADHD.

> Any and all objections are just cries for help to make the decision to buy.
>
> **Subtle Sales Principle No. 5**

Strictly speaking, this may not be true. It could be, for example, that your prospect truly can't afford to buy what you have to offer.

But generally speaking, your prospect is running on autopilot when it comes to parting with cash, especially if it involves big numbers, and that's going to show up as him or her objecting to what you have to offer.

If you view it as a sign to argue, please, pressure, or give up, you are sunk.

If instead you can mentally reframe it as a cry for help, you can stay in that all-important neutral state, pattern interrupt your prospect, and subtly shape them to make the decision you want them to make.

> Empathy for your prospect should be avoided at all costs.
>
> **Subtle Sales Principle No. 6**

Oh my stars and garters.

I can hear the cries of outrage on this one, so let me explain.

There is a strong difference between empathy and caring.

Empathy means you actually and actively feel what your prospect is feeling.

You don't just identify what they are feeling. You identify with it, and wind up going there for yourself.

This is deadly to your need to maintain your frame as the leader of the transaction as the prospect becomes the emotional leader.

Now note again I didn't say you shouldn't care about your prospect's outcome or even like them as a person.

And I'm certainly saying not you should be a schmuck, to use a scientific term.

What I am saying is that it is a profoundly powerful skill to see where your prospect is at, without having to go there for yourself.

If you dip your toe in the emotional waters of your prospect, ok. That can be very useful and even fulfilling for you, emotionally.

Just don't jump into the pool head first and sink to the bottom.

> Subtly confusing your prospect, at the right place and time, can be powerfully effective.
>
> **Subtle Sales Principle No. 7**

This Principle may at first seem to contradict the old axiom about "making the message clear."

But as you will see in the advanced techniques and tools section of this book, there is a time and place to confuse your prospect.

Alright: now that we've given you "the place upon which to stand" it's time to get to the big lever: the tools, both beginning and advanced. See you in Part III.

Artfully and subtly confusing your prospect at the right time and place is a powerful way to pattern-interrupt them and create a temporary window of suggestibility through which you can climb.

The difference between the right word and the wrong word is the difference between the lightning and the lightning bug.

— Mark Twain

Part III

The Basic Building Blocks and Tools of Subtle Selling

Chapter 5
Commands and Suggestions

Before we begin learning the basic tools that will powerfully form the foundation of your subtle selling, it's important to remember that *these tools are meant to be used together*.

It bears repeating that these tools are also the building blocks of the extraordinarily powerful methods and techniques I'll be teaching you in the next section of this book, so you will definitely see them repeated there as well.

Remember too, as I stated in the introduction to this book, *these patterns are meant to be spoken*, so as you read along, speak them out loud several times.

Commands and Suggestions: The Foot Soldiers in Your Subtle Persuasion Army

Let me begin with a story that you may already know, to illustrate the power of commands and suggestions.

According to myth and legend, thousands of years ago, the Greeks and the Trojans fought a war.

The city-state of Troy was surrounded by an impenetrable wall, and despite every effort to breakthrough, the besieging Greek armies could not breach these defenses and take the city.

So the clever Greeks came up with a winning tactic.

They built a gigantic, hollow horse and, beating a hasty retreat, left it at the gates of the city as a gift to the seemingly victorious Trojans.

Unbeknownst to the Trojans, concealed inside the horse were elite shock troops: the cream of the crop of the Greek soldiers.

Once the horse was within the city walls, the hidden Greek soldiers waited until the wee hours of the morning before they poured out, and opened the gates to the city, allowing the Greek armies to take the sleeping Trojans by surprise and sack the city.

When it comes to subtle persuasion, embedded commands and suggestions are the elite soldiers you will hide in your communication to bypass the walls of conscious recognition, thereby nullifying the possibility of detection and resistance.

What Embedded Commands Do

Embedded commands:

- Tell your prospect an action to take. "Sign now, John"
- Tell your prospect feelings to feel. "Feel excited about this agreement" (Remember we are selling decisions and good feelings about decisions!)
- Tell your prospect thoughts to think, "Think this is the best decision you have ever made."

Here are two examples. To make it easy for you, I've **bold-faced** the commands.

"As you **feel better** and better about your ability to **use embedded commands**, you might **get excited** about how you will **use them in your daily life**."

"As you **think about using embedded commands**, and **imagine how good you will feel using them**, you might think "**wow, this something I have to master.**"

Now, do you see how much more subtly powerful this is compared to directly telling you what to think, feel, and do?

Suppose for a moment I simply said, "You are going to feel better and better using embedded commands and you are going to get excited and use them in your daily life."

You'd likely feel ordered about, see me as a jerk, and tell me to take a hike.

Embedding allows us to be subtle instead of confrontational.

Stacking Commands

It's very important to *recognize that the power of commands multiply when you stack them together*.

To use a somewhat violent metaphor, it's like being a boxer.

If you throw one punch a round, no matter how accurate or powerful, you'll likely lose.

You have to throw as many as you can, as the effect of one adds to the effect of the previous one and sets up the power of the next one.

Let's take an example of something I taught in a training seminar for a medium size mortgage brokerage.

"Mr. Smith, I just want to say that I wouldn't want you to **refinance today** unless you **totally understand** why this is the best choice for you. So let's look at the numbers in a way where you can **understand that's true.**"

Here we have a punch straight to the unconscious mind of Mr. Smith.

We are subtly commanding him what to do, and how to think about the action we want him to take.

(There's much more going on in that paragraph, including the use of tools we haven't yet discussed, so we'll be returning to this paragraph multiple times).

Embedding allows us to be subtle instead of confrontational.

Suggestions: Kissing Cousins to Commands

Suggestions are similar to commands, yet differ in being even more subtle, and perhaps more powerful.

Fundamentally, suggestions give the unconscious mind of your prospect an overall meaning picture to put on the transaction (trance-action) you want them to make.

Let's look at the paragraph we just used, but this time I'll mark out the suggestion in bold-face, instead of the commands.

"Mr. Smith, I just wanted to say that I wouldn't want you to refinance today unless you totally understand why **this is the best choice for you**. So let's look at the numbers in a way where you can understand that's true."

Do you see how the suggestion reinforces the commands and puts an overlay of meaning for the entire conversation?

Also notice we are not telling Mr. Smith just exactly how he'll totally understand it's the best choice for him, or when, or why.

We leave it up to his own imagination to fill in the blanks.

Remember one of our core principles: *whatever we can get the prospect to imagine for themselves will be perceived by them as being their own thought, and therefore will not be resisted.*

How to Formulate Suggestions

Suggestions take the form of:

This is x.	This is the best choice for you.
	This is easy for you to decide.
That's x.	That's happening.
	That's taking place.
	That's what's happening.
	That's what's taking place
A great x is y.	A great decision is being made. (My favorite!)

Check out this example that includes commands and suggestions. I've boldfaced the **commands** and italicized the *suggestions*.

"Mr. Jones, I just want to say that I think the more certain you become that *this is the best choice for you,* the better you'll feel when you **sign this contract**. I think that's how a person can recognize *a great decision is being made.*"

Something Super-Subtle

You will notice in this example that we are once again being very vague, allowing Mr. Jones to fill in the blanks with his own imagination.

We are not saying the reasons why Mr. Jones will be certain that it's the best choice for him to sign the contract.

We're not saying in what ways he'll become aware of this or even when.

At every level, his own unconscious mind fills in the blanks for him.

In effect, he is doing 90% of the work.

Finally, take note of the wonderful suggestion that I teach my clients to use as often as possible:

"A great decision is being made."

That suggestion *reinforces the command to sign the contract, by giving our prospect's unconscious mind the reassurance and certainty that signing the contract is a great action for him to take.*

Chapter 6
Presuppositions

Before we get to the gold nuggets of this chapter, I'm not sure just how naturally and easily you'll find yourself feeling very excited as you begin to grasp just how amazingly presuppositions work.

But as that's naturally and easily taking place, let's move forward with our exploration of this amazing tool.

What Presuppositions Do

As with any tool, when you understand what it is designed to do, you naturally use it with much greater impact and success.

Presuppositions serve the purpose of massively increasing the power of your commands and suggestions, by a factor of at least 3 to 4 times.

How is this possible?

It's actually quite simple.

Presuppositions powerfully imply and amplify the notion that the commands and suggestions you give are powerful, true, and irresistible.

Once your presuppositions subtly slide into your conversations, your prospect's unconscious mind *must and will accept the truth of your commands and suggestions.*

Presuppositions powerfully imply and amplify the notion that the commands and suggestions you give are powerful, true, and irresistible.

Notice the difference in the power of these two examples.

I'll leave out the presuppositions from the first example and then add them to the second.

"Mr. Smith, I just want to say you that it's great that you can feel good about your decision to move ahead today, because I think you can see it's a great choice to make."

Now let's change it around a bit and add in some presuppositions (which I've **bold-faced** and which I will unpack shortly).

"Mr. Smith, I just want to say that as you **naturally** and **easily** feel good about your decision to **quickly** move ahead today, it's **equally** great that you can **clearly** see it's a great choice to make."

Now it's no longer a matter of Mr. Smith feeling good. He's naturally and easily feeling good. It's no longer just a matter of him seeing it's a great choice to make. He can now clearly see it's a great choice to make.

Categories of Presuppositions

Adverb presuppositions (by far the most powerful):

- naturally
- easily
- powerfully
- quickly
- effortlessly
- truly
- mysteriously
- totally
- suddenly
- completely
- comfortably

Adjective presuppositions:

- quick
- easy
- fast
- powerful
- powerful
- effortless
- true
- good
- clear

Presuppositions of time:

- as
- while
- after
- before
- while
- now
- when
- later
- until
- today
- has
- had
- has been
- prior
- already
- presently

Presuppositions of awareness:

- imagine
- recognize
- discover
- realize
- think
- recall
- picture
- notice
- become aware
- see

Practical Example:

Here is a word for word example I created for the phone sales team of a mortgage brokerage house I trained:

"Mr. Smith, before we quickly lock in this rate today, I just want to say that you might be surprised at how naturally and easily you can see a great decision's being made. I think that's part of the process when you recognize it's safe to move ahead now."

So, in this example we have:

presuppositions of time:

- before
- quickly
- today
- now

presuppositions of awareness:

- see
- recognize

and adverb presuppositions:

- quickly
- naturally
- easily

Also notice how we are using our old friend from previous examples, the embedded suggestions.

What are they in this example?

- a great decision's being made
- it's safe to move ahead now

Now, as you take a moment to clearly see the momentum you create when you use these tools together, how naturally and easily can you recognize how powerful it is as you use these tools together?

To use a metaphor, when you use just one or two tools, it's like tossing a few snowballs at giant mountain.

A little "poof," a bit of spray, and they're gone forever.

When you use the tools in concert, it's like finding the weak point in the mountain and rolling one snowball down at just the right place, in just the right way, so it gathers enough momentum and mass to…

Create A Subtle Persuasion Avalanche!

Here's another great example I came up with just now, and you'll really find yourself loving it, because you can use it in virtually any business in response to the question, "Why should we pick/go with/hire your firm?"

Here we go:

"Well, Mr. Smith, I wouldn't expect you to discover your own reasons to go with us until you strongly recognize that feels powerfully good and right for you. After all isn't that the only way a person can see a great decision is going to be made?"

Now, this is just loaded with good—make that great—subtle and powerful chains of suggestions, commands, presuppositions and *lots of lovely vague language.*

So much is left to Mr. Smith to fill in the blanks for himself, that you will often discover that it creates the illusion that you were describing in detail to him exactly what he is looking for when it fact *you didn't say one damned specific word or give one tiny iota of a specific reason why he should hire you.*

I call this creating the *illusion of authority.*

Remember: *a potential client will not trust you are an authority on* **where they should go** *until they* **trust you are an authority on where they are at**.

And paradoxically, the best way to do that is to not try to be an authority at all.

In fact, counter to common wisdom and everything else you've been taught before, the more you throw reasons, details and facts to try to prove yourself to Mr. Smith, the more you weaken your position by appearing to be just like every other shmoe who is down on his knees trying to win his business.

Don't toss a persuasion snowball, create a subtle persuasion avalanche!

When you use artfully vague language as illustrated in the prior example, you're not only using the leverage and power of Mr. Smith's own imagination. *You're also creating the frame that you're a person who Mr. Smith can trust and a person who doesn't need to beg for Mr. Smith's business.*

What does this boil down to?

Just this: *Right out of the chute, you are creating the frame that you are the one that holds the value in the transaction, not Mr. Smith.*

Right from the very beginning and throughout the rest of the transaction, **_you_** *get to be in the power position*, **before** you even present the details of your proposal/proposition/offer etc.

I want you to stop and think about the power of that one principle, put into practical play in your business.

What if, *within the first few minutes of the transaction*, you can establish the frame within the unconscious mind of your prospect that you are the one who holds the value?

If all you took from this book was that *one ability alone*, how would that fundamentally and radically transform your entire business?

Of course, there will come a time in the transaction when the numbers have to be explained and put on the table.

But the trick is to do that only *after* you've positioned yourself as the one in the power position and the one holding the value in your prospect's mind.

Is this counter-intuitive?

You bet.

Does it contradict everything you've been taught before about "making the message clear?"

Damn straight.

Will it make you a ton of money and have you biting your cheeks at how easy it is?

On my cats' bushy tails, I swear it will.

So remember: *be vague and establish your position of authority and value in your prospect's mind before you present the numbers and details.*

Be vague and establish your position of authority and value in your prospect's mind before you present the numbers and details.

Chapter 7
Subtle Setup Phrases

Remember that our aim in using commands, suggestions, and presuppositions is to *shape our prospect's decisions outside of their conscious awareness.*

Subtle Setup Phrases are fantastic ways to create our conversational framework so we accomplish just that.

Let's give a practical example that I created for a client in the financial services industry (you can read a transcript of an actual training I did with him in the first bonus section at the end of this book).

His biggest challenge was "onboarding" clients: a technical way of saying getting them to come into the office.

I taught him to use the subtle setup phrase that is my absolute favorite: "If you were to."

Here it is, word for word:

"**If you were to** come into the office this week, I can't be the one to say when might be the best time to do that. I can do x, y and z. **If you were to** pick one now, which do you think works best?

Can you now naturally see how easily this subtle setup phrase allowed my client to slip in the commands to "come into the office this week" and to "pick one now"?

Here is a list of my favorite subtle setup phrases:

- if you were to
- if I were to
- you find
- you might find
- you don't need to
- you might find that you
- you could
- you may
- you might
- how easily you
- allow you to
- you can
- can you
- a person can
- a person might
- a person could

Let's give you another example:

"Mr. Jones, I just want to say that if you were to move forward with this today, I only want that to happen because you find this truly makes sense for you. So please feel free to ask the questions that **allow you to** recognize that's happening."

The Real Power of This Language

There is something even more subtle and powerful going on with that last paragraph, that once again has to do with *the frame we are setting on the transaction and how we are defining the meaning of our relationship with Mr. Smith.*

Rather than seeming to be a pushy or desperate salesperson, we are cleverly and subtly positioning ourselves as a helpful guide **who is merely there to answer the questions that Mr. Smith needs to ask.**

Now, every salesperson who wants to be helpful, or just appear to be, invites a potential client/buyer to ask questions.

They say something like, "Feel free to ask any questions that might come up."

However, notice the difference between that and what we say:

"So please feel free to ask the questions that allow you to recognize that's happening."

Phrased this way, Smith's behavior of asking questions *isn't* just about his wanting more data. It also is *a subconscious trigger to <u>repeat and reinforce</u> the chain of suggestions and commands we've just given him.*

In essence, it sets up a "feed-forward loop" using a behavior Mr. Smith is going to do anyway.

As he repeats that behavior of asking questions throughout the transaction, the power of our suggestions and commands continues to grow.

Let me diagram it:

Our initial chain of commands and suggestions ➜ Smith asking questions ➜ Smith unconsciously repeats and reinforces our chain of commands and suggestions ➜ Smith asks more questions ➜ Smith unconsciously repeats and reinforces our chain of commands and suggestions ➜ Smith buys.

Pretty heady stuff, and perhaps a bit troubling when you consider what it says about rational decision making and free will.

If it hasn't shaken you up a bit, you haven't been paying close enough attention because the power of this is very profound and it is almost certainly outside of the realm of anything you've considered before.

So I invite you to pause, take a break, and then re-read this chapter before you go forward. You'll want to make sure your mind is rested and ready, because we are about to roll out the big guns.

Any sufficiently developed technology is indistinguishable from magic.
—Arthur C. Clarke

Part IV

Advanced Tools

Chapter 8
False Profession of Ignorance and Trance Phrases

As salespeople, we want to convey confidence without appearing to be arrogant or a know it all. We want to convey the appearance of authority, not the infliction of authoritarianism.

What if we could do that, and at the same time powerfully set up our prospect's mind to accept our suggestions and commands by dissipating any need to resist or push back against us?

That's where a false profession of ignorance or an "FPI" comes in.

A Word About Context

The false profession of ignorance is never to be used when you present the actual facts and data and/or explain how the numbers work.

Here you want to be absolutely knowledgeable and certain about your answers.

We use the false profession of ignorance when it comes to getting prospects to make decisions.

My favorite FPIs are:

- I can't be the one
- I don't know
- I can't tell

Let's look at a few great examples.

"Mr. Smith, I just want to say that **I don't know** just how exactly you might find yourself wanting to do this. Only you can discover that's happening for reasons that feel totally right for you. "

"Mr. Smith, I'm sure you'll agree that **I can't be the one** to convince yourself now is the time to sign me up as your listing agent. Only you can find your own reasons to do so and only in ways that feel good and right for you."

Trance Phrases

We are also using another extremely powerful advanced tool in the above examples, and that's trance phrases.

Now, don't be scared off by the term "trance."

Your prospect isn't going to drop into a deep sleep and start quacking like a duck.

By trance I mean an absence of conscious agency and/or the surrender of conscious effort in favor of an unconscious and automatic allowing.

Let's look at my absolutely favorite trance phrase, which you might find yourself realizing I've been using throughout this book.

It's "find yourself" as in "find yourself doing x ."

What does it mean to "find yourself" doing something?

Did you ever just "find yourself" reaching in the refrigerator without remembering what you were looking for?

Did you ever just "find yourself" falling in love? Or maybe "find yourself" falling out of love, and wondering what the hell you were thinking?

You may "find yourself" doing, feeling, or thinking something, but the key point I am illustrating is that the phrase "find yourself" describes something that happens as part of our normal human lives. So much of what we do is simply a reaction to what we experience, and that reaction takes place beyond our normal conscious choice and authority.

It can be bruising and even shocking to the ego to accept this reality, but as grown-ups we may as well accept it and use it to our advantage, or it will work against us.

Let's quote one of the previous examples where I was able to use a trance phrase:

"Mr. Smith, I just want to say that I don't know just how exactly you might find yourself wanting to do this. Only you can discover that's happening for reasons that feel totally right for you. "

Another trance phrase I like is "convince yourself."

Now, strictly speaking, the phrase "convince yourself" is grammatically incorrect.

The proper phrasing would be "convince you."

But remember what I said in the principles and axioms section that sometimes confusing your prospect can be a good thing?

When we are grammatically incorrect in a skillful way we create a momentary subtle confusion which, in turn, creates a momentary window of suggestibility through which our commands and suggestions can slide.

Here is an example combining "convince yourself" with my favorite, "find yourself."

"Mr. Smith, I'm sure you'll agree I can't be the one to convince yourself now is the time to sign me up as your listing agent. Only you can find yourself doing so because it naturally and easily makes sense and feels right to you. So please feel free to ask any questions that allow you to recognize that's happening."

Look at what we are doing with poor Mr. Smith's unconscious mind.

- False profession of ignorance
- Trance phrases
- Reframing the meaning of asking questions
- Adverb presuppositions
- Commands and suggestions

Much of what we experience and do as part of our normal human lives happens outside our conscious choice and authority.

Here's another great example utilizing the same tools.

"Mr. Smith, as you are thinking this over, I don't know which of your own thoughts will naturally convince yourself that a great decision is going to be made. But as that's happening, I just want to say I'm so happy to be here to help you find yourself ready to do this."

"When I use a word," Humpty Dumpty said, in rather a scornful tone, "it means just what I choose it to mean, neither more nor less."

— Lewis Carroll

Part V

The Subtle Art of Destroying Objections

Chapter 9
Subtle Power Words and Phrases to Easily Crush Objections

In these next few chapters, I'm going to reveal powerful tools that are easy, fun to use, and will absolutely crush the most common objections you hear.

These work so well, that you may find yourself having to bite your cheeks from laughing out loud.

But before we get to them, I need you to get the principles and concepts that empower the words.

First, it is useful to take on the attitude that any objection from your prospect is just a cry for help to feel good about moving ahead with the buying decision

Now, strictly speaking, this may not be true. An objection could well be an insurmountable statement of an undeniable truth.

Maybe your prospect really is flat broke or really does need to wait for their next paycheck.

But almost always, it isn't true. Rather, it's almost always about something else, and often the prospect won't know what that something else is.

So it's best to take on the attitude that the objection is not the end of the story but merely a punctuation mark in the conversation.

Next, bear in mind that in order to move your prospect where you want them to be, it is necessary to break their pattern.

By this I mean that your prospect, when they offer an objection, is almost always expecting:

- An argument
- Begging in some form or another
- You agreeing to meekly surrender
- You agreeing to let them "think it over" and lamely hand over your card with a pathetic, "Well, call me when you decide."

Now, please don't do that last one. In fact, tattoo this on the inside of your eyelids:

A Sale Delayed Is A Sale Denied

Again, strictly speaking not true, but a great attitude to have.

In any event, when you break your prospect's pattern of expectation, you have, in effect, stopped them in their tracks and given yourself an easy opportunity to switch them to where you want them to go.

Keeping that in mind, let's get to our first method, subtle power words and phrases.

Subtle Power Word: Stop

Let's look at the power of this simple yet subtle word.

When you use the word "stop" it literally commands the prospect to stop thinking in the direction they had been going, and prepare themselves for the suggestion to look at it another way.

Here's a good example.

Let's take a prospect named Tom (because you, like me, are probably tired of our proverbial Mr. Smith).

You are offering up the opportunity for Tom to buy your widget-digit-fragistat.

He raises the "it's a bit out of my budget" objection.

Without skipping a beat, you reply:

"I understand your point, Tom. But if you were to STOP (pause here a moment) and see it in a different way, you might begin to think things differently. With that in mind, why don't we go over these numbers again, so you see how the return on investment is what really matters?"

Now, please note here that we've thrown in multiple commands and suggestions so that the word "stop" is not used in isolation.

They are:

- see it in a different way
- think things differently
- the return on investment is what really matters

Further, the suggestion "think things differently" is both strategically vague and a bit confusing.

Think what things differently? Think about them differently in what way?

All the phrase serves to do is to create confusion but remember that *artfully confusing your prospect at the right moment can have incredible power.*

Why?

Because that moment of confusion and vagueness—that stutter of the mind if you will—creates a wonderful window of receptivity to our chain of commands and suggestions.

Now, to be sure, this "let's go over the numbers and see the return on investment" is a common response to this objection.

But you'll note how doing it in this way creates the pattern interrupt, confusion, and vagueness and therefore the suggestibility that makes the worn-out and stale "look at the return on investment" response suddenly very, very powerful because it is being slid through that window of suggestibility we created.

Subtle Power Phrase: "Up Until Now"

This magic three-word phrase serves to acknowledge that there was a challenge, *but puts the challenge squarely in the past.*

In effect, you are suggesting, but not declaring, the following:

"Yes, that used to be true. But now you will forget it completely and listen to and agree with this new way of looking at it."

Here's a great example:

"Tom, I can see that up until now that's been an important thought for you, and I have to respect that's been so. I'm just wondering what it would be like if we were to look at it in a different way for just a moment."

Did you notice how we reinforce the frame that *the objection is no longer true* and is firmly in the past, by adding in the phrase "that's been" *twice* in the *same* sentence?

Subtle Power Phrase: "The More The More"

This may well be the hardest tool for you to grasp, so bear with me while I explain, right prior to you powerfully enjoying a breakthrough understanding.

Remember, we are seeking to create that momentum for a persuasion avalanche.

"The more, the more" phrase ties one suggested/commanded direction of our prospect's actions, thoughts, and feelings, to the next.

To use a metaphor, think of it is as a railroad bridge that allows the train to move across a gap and accelerate once it has crossed.

The phrase takes this form:

"The more you x, the more you y."

Simple, yes?

Here is a great example I came up with for a real estate company I trained.

It's meant to be used in the context of taking a potential buyer on a walkthrough of a property for sale.

"As we are doing the walk-through of the home today, I think **the more you recognize what you love about it, the more easily you might find this is the right choice for you**. So please feel free to offer up any questions you might have, ok?"

Now, I have to confess I did something else here that borders on unfair, even by my standards.

What was it?

Look at this piece of genius:

"feel free to offer up."

Of course, on the surface, we are giving them permission to ask questions.

Because of the way the sentence is constructed, and the context in which it is said, the unconscious mind also interprets it as "make an offer on the home."

Chapter 10
Agreement Frames

The beauty of agreement frames is how they give your prospect virtual amnesia for their entire way of thinking, and in addition, *use their objection as the very reason they should move forward.*

We appear to be on the prospect's side of things, avoiding even the appearance of pushing back or arguing, while at the same time getting them to see things exactly our way.

Agreement frames start with:

- I agree
- I understand
- I realize

These phrases must be combined with linkage phrases. These take the form of:

- and that's because
- and that means
- and as soon as that happens
- and as soon as I do
- and as soon as you do
- and I might add

Let's look at this little beauty:

Objection: "I'm not ready to buy."

"I agree you aren't ready to buy now, and that's because I haven't helped you to naturally see the value of doing so. And that means that just as soon as I do, you can see it as something you want to for yourself now. Let's give it another look."

Objection: "I need to think it over."

"I agree that getting the clarity you need to feel certain this is a good choice is very, very important, and I agree that's the smart way to do it. And that means as soon as I help clear up whatever was standing in the way, you might be surprised at how good you feel moving forward with this. With that in mind, let's have a look at this a different way."

(Note the subtle use of the word "was" which puts the objection squarely in the past.)

Objection: "It's too expensive."

"I agree it seems too expensive, and that's because we haven't yet gone through the return on investment in a way that will allow you to see this is a truly great choice. And that means as soon as we do, you might feel much more ready to move forward with this."

I would like to point out that in this example, and in the one above it, I've added a "softener" here, which is the word "might."

I almost always use it with the phrase "and that means" because I don't want to run even the slightest chance of getting any pushback from the prospect.

Also notice how we snuck in the word "seems" which, strictly speaking, stands as a subtle power word on its own, as does the word "appears," as they each imply that the objection is only an illusion on the part of the prospect which they can now drop.

Remember, use the tools in combination and they will give you the combination to the safe of your prospect's mind.

Chapter 11
The Redefine Pattern

This subtle pattern is a nuclear weapon in your objection destroying arsenal.

It totally changes the momentum of the conversation with our prospect, and like the agreement frame, gives them a virtual "amnesia" for their objection.

Redefine patterns take the form of:

"The issue isn't x . The issue is y ."

Or:

"It's not about x . It's about y ."

Suppose the objection takes the form of "It's too expensive."

The response could be: "The issue isn't the expense. The issue is that I haven't yet helped you to find your own reasons to clearly see the return on investment is more than worth it. If you were to look at it in just that way, you might discover yourself thinking about it differently. So let's have another look at it so you can feel good moving forward with this."

Notice once again how we are using *multiple tools combined together* to create that "persuasion avalanche."

Allow me to unpack it for you, as follows:

We have the vague trance phrase "find your own reasons."

We have the adverb presupposition "clearly."

The setup phrase "If you were to."

The trance phrase "discover yourself" paired with the vague "thinking about it differently."

And finally, we have our "kill shot": the command "feel good moving forward with this today."

Now, at this point I want to pause to just say that it doesn't matter whether you find yourself feeling pulled forward by your growing excitement to use these tools for your financial abundance, or pushed ahead to use them by your desire to make gobs of money while laughing to yourself at how easy selling will have become.

What matters is how quickly and easily that excitement and desire might cause you to stop and think, "Man, I've got to learn more from Paul Ross. And that means you can feel good when you inquire about hiring me to speak, train or teach as you go to SpeakerPaulRoss.com.

(Sorry. I just cannot resist using these tools everywhere and anywhere. How excited will you be when you find they become second nature and just easily flow from you?)

Another Example That You'll Love

Let's say your prospect says, "I need time to think it over."

Here's a great redefine pattern to crush that objection.

"Maybe the issue isn't time. Maybe the issue is the clarity you need to recognize this really is a great decision. If you were to find yourself, looking at it like that, doesn't it make sense for me to help you feel good about moving forward with this?"

Now, you might have noticed in this case I once again used a "softening" term—in this case "maybe"—to avoid the possibility of any push-back from the prospect due to their perception of me being a "know it all."

Remember: if your prospect views you as a "know it all" they are very likely not going to want to know you at all, and will probably say "no" to it all.

That said, *there is a time and place to drop any softening* and speak with absolute assurance, and that's when you are presenting the numbers, data, parameters etc. of your product, service, and/or the actual offer on the table.

Returning to our examples for meaning redefines, here is a great one for a very common objection. (While it's geared towards real-estate sales, it could just as well apply to any objection on price, expense, or cost.)

Objection: "Your commission is too high."

"The issue isn't my commission appearing high. The issue is how low your expectations are at the price a top negotiator can fetch for your home. At the end of the day, it's the amount of cash you have on the table that counts, and you're not going to get that from someone who would sell themselves out cheap."

Notice Something Else

As if what we are doing in this example isn't powerful enough, I'll point out yet another tool it uses which is *a basic common-sense truism*.

A truism can be defined as a statement that is self-evidently, obviously, and inarguably true. In effect, *it seals up and multiplies the power of all that has come before it.*

And it *is* true that the prospects aren't going to get the best negotiating talent from someone who sells themselves cheap.

The prospect just cannot argue with this. And the real beauty of it is that they tie the truth of the truism (and yes, I'm being redundant here) back to the truth of everything else you've said prior to it.

Here's another example of how we could use a truism for this objection. And just to be really clever we will combine agreement frames and the redefine pattern.

Remember: if your prospect views you as a "know it all" they are very likely not going to want to know you at all, and will probably say "no" to it all.

"Well, Mr. and Mrs. Jones all I can say is **that in life you get what you pay for**. And that means (agreement frame) the issue isn't (meaning redefine) my commission appears too high. The issue (meaning redefine) is your expectation of what a top negotiator can get for your home is too low. And that's because (agreement frame) at the end of the day, getting top dollar for your home is what really matters."

Now you might be thinking, "Wow, Paul. All of these tools being piled on top of each other just seem too complex for me.

My answer is, "The issue isn't the that the tools appear complex. The issue is how exciting it is to realize how easy they will be to apply, as you naturally find yourself using them in the real world. "

Language is a process of free creation; its laws and principles are fixed, but the manner in which the principles of generation are used is free and infinitely varied.

— Noam Chomsky

Part VI

The Bonus Transcripts

Chapter 12

Subtle Words in Action: A Training Session With a Financial Services Professional

Author's note: This bonus section is a transcript of a training session I did with John, one of my VIP clients in the financial services sector.

While it is true that it is a great example of specific applications to his line of business, please bear in mind that the principles and tools apply in any field of selling.

I think you'll enjoy following along with John's learning process in a way that naturally and easily increases your own excitement as you imagine yourself powerfully using what you'll learn.

Paul: What I was saying is that the setup phrases and the embedded commands and the embedded suggestions are the building blocks. They are the glue that holds everything else together. I believe I've given this analogy before. Like the story of the Trojan Horse, we're going to sneak them through. This also requires that we have the right conversational frameworks.

I was saying to someone who's in the real estate business the other day… I'm going to help him create listing presentations because there's a big gap in the real estate training for what you actually say and do when you're doing the walkthrough.

As I said to him, I don't want to take away all the tools that you're already using because you may find some of those are efficacious and they work for you. What I would like you to do—and this is a more difficult task, and I'm here to guide you in it—is to take what you're already doing and slowly begin to incorporate these tools into it.

So rather than thinking of this as a way of removing your confidence or what you're already doing that's working, it's a way to turbocharge what you're already doing so that you get much better results with it.

Just so you know, you're already a very competent, very highly successful, highly motivated individual; I'm not attempting to take any of that away. What I want to do instead is show you how to piggyback onto what you're doing that works.

John: That's so important, what you said, because I'm at a stage where I'm a little bit burning out. I think, with your coaching, I can streamline the process and make the sales funnel a little quicker.

Paul: What we want to do is, as far as possible, shorten the sales cycle. As I've said before—it bears repeating—if you don't direct and influence people's decisions, they're going to default to their autopilot responses because they have what I call cognitive momentum and emotional inertia. If you aren't the one directing those decisions and ways of thinking, they're just going to default to what they've already done.

That ultimately not only doesn't serve you, but it doesn't serve them. If, as I think as true in your case, you really are offering superior service—if not superior products—then you're doing them a disfavor by not doing the influencing, by not doing the persuading. I'm sure that's not how you want to go about doing things.

John: Very well said. You're exactly right. That's very well said. Beautiful.

Paul: Great. Fantastico.

What I want to do is go through commands and suggestions again.

Paul: The reason why we're embedding suggestions and commands is that we want to enter the unconscious mind of the prospect and bypass conscious resistance. That way, we nullify the possibility of being detected. Remember, if we're detected, then people are going to go, "Take a hike."

Here's what commands do. A command will tell a person an action to take. For example, "Sign this contract." It will tell a person what feelings to feel: "Feel excited about this agreement." It will tell a person what thoughts to think: "This is something I want to do."

By the way, I want to make a point very clear. "Think this is something you want to do." I'm not pointing it out in this part of my manuscript because there's an advanced understanding. "Think this is something you want to do."

You'll notice we're not saying exactly what that something is. I'm not saying, "Think that signing this contract is something you want to do." I'm not saying, "Think that coming into the office today is something you want to do," or "Think that referring to people to me is something that you want to do."

Now, there are going to contexts in which you are going to want to directly spell out what they want to do, but we're not being specific here—later on, I'll show why that is—because given the right context and the right setup, when you're non-specific, people are going to fill in the blank with the action you want them to take.

This goes back to one of the key axioms, which is whatever you can get a person to imagine for themselves will be perceived by them as being their own thought and therefore they won't resist it. If you have to give facts, data, figures, information, direct commands, even if it's in their own interest, people will often resist it.

One of the things that I'm sure as a professional salesperson, you've noticed is that a lot of times people just can't recognize what's in their best interest. Does that make sense? If people always recognized immediately that you are the person to go with, that your product is superior, that your service is superior, there would be no need to sell.

John: Got it.

Paul: Now I'm going to give you some examples, and then what I want to do is work them into specific examples for what you're doing. Okay?

What I've done is marked out the embedded commands in boldface. Here we go. "As you feel better and better about your ability"—this is a command to feel something. "As you feel better and better about your ability to use embedded commands"—that's telling an action to take—"you could think about all the ways you could use them in daily life." So, "As you feel better and better about your ability to use embedded commands, you could think about all the ways you could use them in daily life."

Here's an example of being a little bit vague. I'm not saying, "Think about using them with your wife. Think about using them with your kids." I'm asking them to think about all the ways they could use them in daily life.

So these are—in a sense—what I would call deep-dive suggestions or commands. They really require an active working of the imagination, of the unconscious.

One of the things Dr. Milton Erickson said—he is really the founder of NLP and everything else—is that the unconscious is always listening. It's always active, always listening, always working, and it's always receptive to commands and suggestions, particularly when we create the right environment to be receptive.

Here's another one. "As you think about using embedded commands and begin to imagine using them, I'm not sure just how much you'll feel good when you use them."

Let me give you one more. Let's take a situation where your prospect is at the crucial moment of signing a contract. Remember, we're always selling decisions and good feelings about the decisions. I'm not in any way putting down what you do personally or the quality of what you're offering. My view is that people just don't know how to make decisions, particularly about anything about investing money, where they might lose the money. In this example, we're going to embed the commands to sign the contract and feel really good about it.

Also, when people feel really good about doing something, it has two benefits. Number one, they're far more likely to send you referrals. Number two, they're not going to F*&k you up and put you on Yelp. This is the Yelp generation. Back when I was growing up, we didn't have Yelp. A person is nine or ten times more likely to give a bad review than they are a good one.

By the way, do you have a mechanism in place to encourage people to Yelp or to manage your Yelp?

John: No, we don't actually have any Yelp thing, which is good, I think.

Paul: It's a good thing you don't have it? Okay. I'll let that go. You know your business better than I do.

So here we go. "Before you sign this contract, Mr. Jones, I just want to say I feel really proud I've helped you feel good to do that." "I just want to say I feel really proud." This is a really important type of command. "I just want to say I feel really proud." Even though I'm talking about my feelings, it's really way of giving a command for them to feel a certain way.

John: That's interesting. Wow.

Paul: Yes. This is very powerful. In NLP, they call it a switched referential index. I don't like to use NLP jargon. I like to call it the I-you shift.

If I said to you, "John, as we continue to learn together, I feel so pleased that we're continuing to do that," as I talk about my feelings, I'm really giving you the command to feel that.

John: That's interesting. Wow.

Paul: That's called the switched referential index.

John: Where is the switch happening?

Paul: Ah, very good. "I just want to say I feel really proud." When you lean on the command, they're going to hear "feel really proud."

John: Because I'm feeling proud.

Paul: Exactly. "I've helped you to feel good to do that."

Generally speaking, I don't like to give hard and fast rules when we're playing with the human mind, but once I give an action command, particularly one I would call—forgive the technical jargon—a tertiary action command, a command that gets them to finally do what you want them to do, I always want to add in some suggestion that they're going to feel good about it.

I don't know. In your business, do you get buyer's remorse?

John: Not much, to be honest, because they don't have anything tangible in their hand. It's a portfolio I made for them. It's something intangible. But what does happen is that they sign up for something and then look at something else.

To give an example, someone has a bond portfolio, which is very conservative, and they're looking at the stock market and they say, "Hey. The stock market is doing well. But there's a gap." I tell them, "Hey. The reason why we have bonds is because you don't want to lose money and make some income." It's a whole different ballgame. One is ultra-conservative. With the stock market, you can make more money, but you take risks. Sometimes there's a disconnect there.

Paul: I'm wondering how we would play with that. So they'll come back to you and say, "Wait a minute. The stock market is going up"?

John: Yes. It's like comparing oranges and apples. It's a whole different thing. With one, the reason is to preserve your money and generate some income with it. The other one is more for capital appreciation, but it comes with a lot of risks. You can lose half the money. They cannot compare them because that's not what our strategy is. That's a totally different thing.

Paul: In that case, do you have a comeback for them?

John: Yes. I say, "Hey. This is, when we had the meeting, your goal. You don't want to lose the money, but you want to make at least 3% or 4% interest income, and you want to make sure that you get that income and you're not exposed to the market. Are you talking about the stock market, where you can lose half the money? That's not you. That is a whole different goal." So I have to do a job of telling them, "Hey. This is what your goal is, and that's why we did this."

Paul: Which brings me back to the point that it's really important to paint a clear picture.

John: To set the foundation is very important.

Paul: Yes. To set the foundation and also manage expectations. To inoculate them and say, "Now, it's really important that we stick to this structure. From time to time, there may be temptations. There may be something that suddenly pops up that appears to have a higher yield. But remember…"

This is really clever. This is for when they're in your office. You want to see something really wicked that I put in here? You're having this conversation. You say, "From time to time, you may see something that appears to have a higher yield yet has a much higher risk, but remember, when that happens, you're looking for something really safe and secure that you can continue to trust in."

Do you see what you're doing? Are you talking about the investment or talking about yourself?

John: Yourself.

Paul: Exactly. When you're given more than one meaning, the unconscious mind will do what's called—I hate the NLP jargon—a trans derivational search. It will look for all possible meanings and assign both meanings.

I want to give that to you again. The idea here is that when they come to you and say, "Wait. I'm seeing the stock market go up. I want something else," what you want to do is say, "Look, I know this appears tempting to you. Up until this moment, it may have seemed like it had a higher yield, but remember, you're looking for something safe that you can continue to place your trust in."

"Remember, you are looking for something safe that you can continue to place your trust in." And you're doing what we call a personal anchor. You're anchoring those suggestions to yourself, even though it appears like you're talking about the investment.

The mind will say, "I trust the investment. I trust this guy who's talking to me." It will tie the trust in each together, so each feeds the other. So the more they trust you, the more they trust the investment. The more they trust the investment, the more they trust you, which is not a bad outcome, I would say.

Remember, you're not selling your products or services; you're selling decisions and good feelings.

Stacking commands. In classical hypnosis, there's what we call the law of compound suggestion. What this means is if I'm doing therapeutic work with someone, if I give one suggestion, the next suggestion I give increases the power of the prior suggestion. And the suggestion that I give after that increases the power of the previous two suggestions.

What we're doing here is creating a momentum inside the prospect's mind—or inside the patient or client's mind if you're doing therapeutic work—so they're not just going in the direction but they're stepping on the gas.

I had a mentor who was the first person to teach me this stuff. Not a particularly nice guy, but he knew what he was talking about. This guy said, "In the beginning, my job is to get someone on the highway. Then I want to get them in the right lane, and then—the most important part—I want them to step on the gas."

If all you do is give a couple of suggestions, the car is going to stop. Then you're going to turn on the ignition again and then turn it off and then turn it on again. You want to keep that momentum going. The way you keep the momentum going is by stacking commands.

This is an example I created for a mortgage company, but I would like to, if possible, workshop one directly for you word-for-word. Here's the thing with the mortgage company. Generally, a lot of the people who were calling in were what my client called "shoppers." I don't know that this is the case with you, but they're actually talking multiple people at the same time.

John: Which is good. No.

Paul: You don't have that challenge, but he had that challenge. Can I show you this example anyway?

John: Absolutely. Yes, please.

Paul: Okay. I had the loan officers say the following: "I just wanted to say I wouldn't want you to refinance today unless you totally understand why this is the best choice for you So let's look at the numbers before we lock in this rate."

This one has several tools, and you'll see the tools reappearing as we continue training together. I'm going to point those out, if you don't mind. "I just wanted to say" is an example of what we call quotes. Quotes enable you to take suggestions, or anything you want to say for that matter, and embed them even deeper because, essentially, you're not saying it directly.

If I said, "Well, Mr. Smith, I wouldn't you to refinance today unless you totally understand why this is the best choice for you," it doesn't have the same amount of power." By using quotes, we are taking a step back, and in taking that step back, the prospect mentally goes, "Ah. Okay. They're not saying it to me directly."

I've used this in personal altercations. A neighbor once said to me, "Shut your mouth and just open up for what I have to say." I'm not going to say that directly. We're going to go through that later.

I'm wondering. Is there a situation in your own specific business where we might be able to stack some commands?

John: Yeah, absolutely.

Paul: Give me that situation. What we'll do is write it out for you, word for word.

John: Like you said, there are a lot of clients who have been procrastinating. I have a lot of solutions for them. They should go into some kind of managed account or managed solutions, which can help them to manage their portfolio. But because of the cost structure or fee structure, they're hesitant.

They're saying, "Oh, it's a 1% fee," but they're not realizing they're giving up 5% or 6% upside. At the end of the day, you have to make more money if someone is managing your portfolio, managing the risk. So my goal is to understand them and help them. Don't think about the fees, really, but look at the bottom line. It's going to help you make that money.

I don't mind if someone is charging me $1000 if I'm getting $10,000 at the end of the day, because if you were to do it on your own, you would just make $2000. But people just have the concept "Hey, why should I pay? I should for free stuff, or I should look for the cheapest thing."

That's the hurdle I have. I know in my heart I'm doing the right thing, but some people are just born in a certain way. They don't believe in just paying for services.

Paul: This is wicked. I really cackle to myself like a mad scientist. Can you tell I'm really on today?

John: Yes, absolutely. Thank you so much.

Paul: "I can't be the one to realize at the end to the day, it is the money you have in your pocket that counts." The command is "realize at the end of the day, it's the money you have in your pocket that counts." That's the realization you want them to have. You see?

"You're the only one who can recognize that it's not the fees; it's the financial gain." By the way, this is a suggestion. We'll get to this in a second. "It's not the fees; it's the financial gain." We're going to get to suggestions in a second.

"And as I am sure you can imagine, I don't know how quickly you can feel good"—this is really wrong; I'm going to add this to my book—"and allow yourselves to see it this way." This is really wicked. I won't mention you, but I'm adding it to the book.

Let's go through this. What I'm about to show you in this paragraph, I'm actually putting several techniques within it. "I can't be the one to realize at the end of the day, it is the money that you have in your pocket that counts." This is what we call a truism. Would you please write down the word "truism"?

A truism is a statement that is indisputable, that is true in and of itself, or also is a typical slogan that people are raised to believe, like "A stitch in time saves nine," or "A penny saved is a penny earned." People are trained to believe that's true. And "Don't judge a book by its cover."

If I really want to mess with people, do you know what I do? I take two equal and oppositely true truisms and I oppose them. Which is more true? "Don't judge a book by its cover" or "If it looks like a duck and quacks like a duck, it's a duck"? You can watch their brains fry.

"At the end of the day, it's the money you have in your pocket that counts"—this bit is a true statement. They can't disagree with that. How can they say, "No, I don't want more money"? It's a statement about the reality that has to be true. Do you get it?

When you say, "You're the only one who can recognize that" it's making them feel like, "Oh, wait a minute. He's not trying to put any pressure on me by trying to convince me. He's saying it's up to me to recognize that," even though in reality you're giving them a command to recognize it.

"It's not the fees; it's the financial gain." I'm overwhelming you because I'm delivering value here.

John: This is the most beautiful statement I've ever heard in one paragraph. It's unbelievable.

Paul: Which one?

John: Everything. The whole paragraph is just mind-blowing.

Paul: That's why I want to take lots of time to go through this, so if we need it, we'll go 10 or 15 minutes extra.

"You're the only who can recognize it's not the fees; it's the financial gain." This is also not only a truism, which it is, and also a suggestion—we'll get to that; you'll see it momentarily when we get to suggestions—but it's also a meaning reframe. It's taking what they thought was important and saying, "No, that's not what's important. It's the amount of money I'm going to make you that's important." It's called a meaning reframe.

There are several ways to do meaning reframes—a lot of different ways. Let me give you one in your personal life. Let's say you come home and for whatever reason, you had a bad day and you yell at your spouse. She says, "When you yell at me, that means I can't trust you." One meaning reframe would be to say, "So, when I'm vulnerable enough to reveal what I'm truly feeling in the moment, that means you should trust me less?"

Do you see the meaning reframe there? She's saying yelling means you can't be trusted. You're saying yelling means you're being totally vulnerable and sharing your truth. See that meaning reframe?

This is actually an advanced pattern: "It's not the X; it's the Y." We'll get to that later. It's a more advanced tool.

"You're the only one who can recognize it's not the fees. It's the financial gain," which is totally true, by the way. It's not only a truism. You believe this to be true, correct?

John: Yes.

Paul: "And as I'm sure you can imagine, that only comes from professional management of your finances." So you're telling them, "Imagine that only comes from professional management of your finances," which reinforces the truism and realizes the truism "at the end of the day, it's the money that counts." They're all reinforcing the same idea.

Remember how I said that the first one is reinforced by the second one, which is reinforced by the third one? When you do this, it's not the add. It's not like if you get five points of influence through the first one and five points of influence from the second and five points of influence of the third, that would be 15. They multiply. Five times five is 25. You're the math guy. 25 times 5 is…

John: 125.

Paul: So you have 125 points of influence.

John: That's wonderful.

Paul: "I don't know how quickly you can feel good to let yourself see it this way." Now you're not only putting all these suggestions and reframes and truisms in their head but you're telling them to feel good and you're telling them to see it that way.

John: Wow.

Paul: There's virtually no resistance to using this. There's nothing they can do. People say to me, "Won't you get caught?" I've used this stuff on certified master practitioners of NLP, hypnosis, clinical psychologists. They don't get it.

John: This paragraph is a masterpiece.

Paul: When I'm on, when I'm in full-blown hair-on-fire teaching mode, I kick ass. I want you to make sure that you keep this paragraph.

Subtle Words That Sell

The assignment I'll give you is, please, when you get that objection, try it out word for word. What are they going to say? "No, I don't want to make more money." Right?

John: There's nothing [35:16 inaudible]

Paul: What the hell are they going to say?

John: It's not like we're just making them money. We're going to make them feel good. So there's no objection.

Paul: Right. Exactly. Stack suggestions and commands, meaning reframes, truisms. You see when you take these tools and compound them, there's really no way the person can resist. There just isn't. That's the beauty of this. This is why I really want to get this out there into the market. When I create the platform that helps people hear this and they really get it, I think it's going to explode brains.

Let me do something right away to give you extra-special amazing service so that you know I'm serious about doing so. I'm going to email you this paragraph right now.

John: Thank you. Awesome.

Paul: It's my joy to teach. Would you please check your email to see that you have that?

Paul: That's awesome.

I don't want you to get too focused in on this distinction, but suggestions, how are they different from commands? Well, suggestions are kissing cousins to commands. They take a different form.

Here's what they look like. I'm going to give you the formula, and then I'm going to give you some word-for-word examples, and then I want to go back to our previous examples and show you where the suggestions are. Okay?

They take the form of "This is x ," as in, "This is easy," or "This is the best choice for you." You're telling people how to feel about the overall direction that you're taking them.

Here's an example. "Mr. Jones"—and I'm only emphasizing the suggestions—"I think the more certain you become that this is the best choice for you, the better you'll feel when you sign this contract." "Sign this contract" is the command.

"But I only want you to do that because you clearly see how much this is the best choice for you." So I'm repeating "this is the best choice for you" twice. "This is easy for you to realize." Remember, "This is _x_ ," "This is the best choice for you," "This is easy," "This is easy for you to realize."

Going back to the examples we've given, we didn't have too many examples there, but did you get the point?

Another form suggestions take is "That's _x_ ," "It's _x_ ," "_x_ is _y_ ," and "_x_ are _y_ ." Let me unpack that for you so that you get total clarity and you really get it. For instance, I could say to you, "As you, dear student, realize that suggestions are easy and fun to use…" That's the "_x_ are _x_ " form. X is "suggestions" and "fun and easy to use" is the Y. I can say to you, "As you, dear student, realize that suggestions are easy and fun to use, you probably can think it's a snap to use suggestions. Maybe you can smile to yourself as you recognize that."

Here's my favorite form: "That's _x_ / It's _y_ ." These two I layer in all the time. "As you, dear student, realize that suggestions are easy and fun to use…" – x are y – "…you probably can think it's a snap to use suggestions. – x is y – "Maybe you can smile to yourself as you recognize that's happening."

In this form, when we use "that's happening" at the end of a chain of commands, what we're actually doing is taking that whole chain of suggestions and commands and telling them to do it again.

When we say "that's happening," we're saying to the unconscious, "Take that whole chain of suggestions and commands and continue to run that loop through the person's head." So now, we're not only putting suggestions and commands into their head, but the suggestion "that's happening" is causing them to loop on those suggestions and commands.

It's like making it run through their head over and over and over and over. It's like putting our voice in our brain and then continuing to talk. Does that make sense? It's a really powerful way and an easy way to take this elegant chain of commands and suggestions that we've set up and get them to continue to run it in their mind. That's pretty wicked, huh?

John: It is.

Paul: Here's something that goes along with suggestions and goes along with commands. Throughout this, I've been using presuppositions, but let's unpack them so that you can understand how easy they are to use.

As with any tool I teach you, it's very important to understand how the tool is applied. If you know the application of the tool, it becomes much easier to use it powerfully, use it efficiently, use it easily. If you were from Mars and I handed you a hammer and didn't tell you its function, who knows what you'd do with it?

The main purpose of presuppositions is to make anything said after them true, and more importantly, they set up commands and suggestions for delivery. You could say that they're part of what I call a conversational framework. Conversational frameworks help make language patterns appear as normal, ordinary, mundane conversations. You don't want to walk in and say, "Now, Mr. Investor, [45:31 inaudible] to sign the document. Give me the money and give me a referral."

There are several categories of presuppositions. There are, first of all, the adverb/adjective presuppositions. I find that the adverb presuppositions are far more powerful. In fact, I'm only putting in the adjective presuppositions to be completely thorough. I normally never use adjective presuppositions. I don't know anyone who uses them, but to be a thorough, efficient teacher, it's incumbent on me to include them.

Here's a list of the adjective presuppositions: quick, easy, natural, mysterious—these are just some of them—effortless, true, good, fast.

Here's where we really, really hit gold. I could do a whole hour on these alone: quickly, powerfully, easily, and naturally. I'll point out—and we'll go slowly through these—that I like to use these two combined. Using these two combined is my favorite combination.

Could you please write down On a piece of paper "adverb presuppositions"? Then please write down, if you would, "Paul's favorite combination"—man, I'm excited about that paragraph I came up with; that is an advanced one—"easily and naturally." Those are the two that I really love to go together; they fit hand and glove.

Mysteriously, effortlessly, truly, instantly, totally, thoroughly, completely, suddenly, explosively, exponentially, faster.

Presuppositions of time: before, after, as, while, now, later, until, today, has, had, has been, had been, prior, already, presently.

Presuppositions of awareness. I would say these are not only useful, friend, but they're necessary. You can't really use these tools without using them: recognize, discover, remember, think, imagine, picture, recall, realize. Now, just so that you know, I use that one, and I use that one a lot. Those two I use a lot. As we continue the training, I'll unpack these for you. I'll give you practical examples.

John: I just love the word "presupposition of awareness." The word itself is so powerful.

Paul: Yes. Let's look at an example. Again, we'll see if we can work something out for your specific context, but I wrote this for someone in the mortgage business who backed out of the training. He said, "Interest rates are so low I'm hiring monkeys and putting them on the phone." My statement to him was "Wait until interest rates go up, and then you'll see." Then I just left him alone.

Here are the presuppositions. "Mr. Jones, before you feel good about quickly locking in this rate today, you might be surprised at how you can become aware of just how easily that's happening."

Let me go through these for you. The first command here is "feel good." It's a feeling command. I'm saying "Before you feel good." If I say, "Before you feel good," what does that presuppose is going to happen?

John: Maybe that they're not feeling good now?

Paul: No. It presupposes that they're going to feel good. If I said, "Mr. Jones, you feel good about locking in this rate," they may go, "F*&k you. I don't feel good." I'm saying "Before you feel good."

John: So you're basically out the objection also, right?

Paul: Correct. Exactly. You're taking away the objection...

John: The resistance. That's pretty good.

Paul: ...All resistance by using the presupposition. "Before"—is it an adverb/adjective presupposition?

John: No.

Paul: No. It is a presupposition of time. "Before." "Before you feel good about quickly locking in this rate..." We could say, "Before you feel good about locking in this rate..." That's not bad, but "quickly locking in this rate" is doing two things. First of all, it's presupposing they're going to lock in the rate. Then it's telling them to do it quickly.

If I said, "Mr. Jones, before you feel good about slowly locking in this rate today," that's an adverb presupposition, just like "quickly," but do we want them to do things slowly? No. Why don't we slowly? Because the more time they think it over, the more they are likely to become confused.

Write this down. Confusion is your number one enemy to selling. Confusion is more powerful an enemy than distrust or skepticism.

John: Wow.

Paul: Write this one down, and then we'll workshop it. One of my teachers taught me this—my second or third best teacher. A confused mind makes no choices.

The best counter to confusion is clarity and speed. The mind actually likes speed. The longer you give someone to make a decision, the more likely there is that they'll talk themselves out of it. You have to balance that against not pressuring. You have to walk the fine line between getting them to do things speedily but not making them feel pressured. That is the art form. I have to write that down: confusion is the biggest enemy of your sale.

On the other hand—I'm going to give you a contradiction—sometimes you must confuse your client. Sometimes confusion artfully used is incredibly powerful and is a very, very powerful tool.

John: An example?

Paul: We'll get there. It's an advanced tool. I promise you. I'm not teasing you. We'll get there.

So where are the presuppositions here? Well, here's the presupposition of time. Here's the adverb presupposition—"quickly"—and here's another adverb presupposition—"easily." "You can become aware of just how easily"—remember our favorite suggestion—"that's happening."

Let's go through this again and show you what else is really powerful here. "Mr. Jones, before you feel good about quickly locking in this rate…" Notice what we're not saying: "Mr. Jones, before you feel good about quickly locking in this rate today because you see that it's the best rate possible and you can see the return on the investment and you recognize that you don't want to lose out." We're not piling on all the reasons.

"Mr. Jones, before you feel good about quickly locking in this rate today…" We're not telling him why and how he should feel good. We're letting his own mind fill in the blank.

I want you to remember this as a key principle: Whatever you can get someone to imagine for themselves will be perceived as being their own. So we leave in the blank.

Now, there are times when you have to be specific. When you explain exactly how the investment works, you must be specific. You must know your facts and data. You can't hesitate or do any of that. I get that. You know the technical aspect of your business. You could take a year and I still wouldn't understand it. I don't know numbers for shit. I can't even balance a checkbook, and that's an embarrassing truth. I'm not lying to you.

So we're combining presuppositions. There's a presupposition of time, adverb/adjective presupposition, another adverb presupposition. Then we're throwing in that nice suggestion: "that's happening." Remember that the "that's happening" suggestion is a way of taking that whole loop of suggestions and commands and having them run it through their mind again and again.

Look what I'm doing here. "As you review this example and easily find how powerful it is to use these commands, I want to say that before you do that, it's up to you to recognize it's fun to use these tools in combination, isn't it?" So I'm just using the tools just to mess with the reader. You see that?

John: Yes.

Paul: Now, this is a general purpose one. We did a paragraph for you, but I also like to general-purpose these. Mr. X is your prospect. "Well, Mr. X, I wouldn't expect you to easily discover your own reasons to go with us until you strongly recognize that feels powerfully good and right for you. So let's have a look at some of these numbers before that happens."

Let me go through this. Let me explain why and how this would be useful for you. "Mr. X, I wouldn't expect you to easily discover your own reasons…" See the presupposition? This is an adverb presupposition.

Now, this is an advanced tool, but I'm going to go over it here, and then we'll revisit it when we get into more advanced tools. "Discover your own reasons." This is what I call a deep-dive command. If I unpacked it and I said to him directly, I would say, "Mr. X, I'm going to command you to go inside your unconscious mind, go into a trance, and come up with all the reasons why you want to do this. On the count of three: 1, 2, 3, go!"

If I did it exactly like that, what would Mr. Jones do?

John: If you do say this, he will object.

Paul: He'll tell me to get lost. I would hope he would kick me in the butt.

So, "Mr. X, I wouldn't expect you to easily discover you own reasons"—we're telling him to go inside his mind and come up with his own reasons—"to go with us until you strongly recognize"—see the word "strongly"; there's your adverb presupposition—"that feels powerfully good and right for you. So, let's have a look at some of these numbers before that happens." So we're saying it's going to happen.

What I like about this chain of commands and suggestions is that it's very vague. I'm not saying "Look, the reason you're going to go with us because you're going to see that I'm the best salesperson and this is the best investment and it's going to give you the best rate of return."

Don't get me wrong. When you're presenting the actual numbers, then you can say, "Here's why it's going to give you the best rate of return, the best safety, the best this." But you want to preface it with this.

Before you take them through the numbers, you want to set up that frame of mind that they essentially have already made the decision to go with you. If you're setting up the frame of mind that they're ready, as you present the facts and figures and numbers, they're going to think, "Yeah. I want to go with this. I want to go with this. I want to go with this. I want to go with this." It's much more likely, in that frame of mind, that the numbers will feel good to them.

Now, I'm not taking away from the need to make the numbers make sense.

John: It's super powerful—that paragraph—too.

Paul: Yes. What I like about it is you can purpose it into any business you're doing. You could do it if you're selling multi-level marketing. You could do it if you're selling cars.

Now I want to get to setup phrases and setup words. How are you doing with this? Are you feeling overwhelmed or is this going at a good pace?

John: Yes, it's good. Powerful, super good.

Paul: Awesome. Bingo, bingo, bingo. Setup phrases and setup words. Setup phrases are another way to conversationally set up commands and suggestions.

We'll send you the video, and then I'm going to pass it on immediately to my ops manager to pass it on to MagiScript. You have my personal phone number, do you not?

John: Yeah, I do.

Paul: All right. If you don't get it in seven days, call me. They have a turnaround time, usually, of seven to ten days. This time, I want to make sure you're so happy you're pissing in your pants and have a boner.

You'll notice that the setup phrases incorporate the presuppositions. Let me go through these with you: how easily you, how clearly you, how powerfully you, I don't know if you can…

John: Do you suggest I make something like this? I write out the setup phrases so it's always in front of my eyes—to memorize it and internalize it. All right?

Paul: Yes. Immersion. One of the things you could do is listen to the audio from the video over and over and over and over again.

John: Yes, I can save the video and listen over again.

Paul: So: a person doesn't need to, you might find that you, you only find that you, I can't say how, I can't be the one to, you might, you could, you may, a person might, a person could.

These last five—we will get to them in the next training—are what I call softeners. Now, already we're going to remove any resistance, but softeners are a way—when you're delivering something particularly powerful—to soften it and make sure there really, really is no resistance. They'll not only take away resistance but they'll take away any need to resist.

Here's a practical example using setup phrases to onboard a client prospect. I'm working with a young guy who's in a business similar to yours. He said, "The number one problem we have in our office"—and it's a small office, by the way—"is getting people to come into the office when we want to onboard them. It's the most effective way to get them to do things—to get the contract signed, to understand the investment, or whatever."

I don't know if that's something you do in your business or not.

John: Yes. Onboarding is not a problem. I have a lot of leads and lot of clients. The key part is for me to move them from non-paying to paying, so move them to management. That's the thing I do, pretty much. The other way, I have so many clients I can't even handle it.

Paul: Well, that's a good problem to have.

John: Yes. It's a good problem.

Paul: Hopefully, one day as I keep pushing this, I'll have that, too. I'm sure I will. It's just a matter of time.

In this example—and we'll close up with this example—we're not only going to command that the client come to the office but we're going to get him to say what time that'll be. Watch how this works. Ready?

"If you were to" – there's the setup phrase.

John: "If you were to" is in the hall of fame. I love that.

Paul: Yeah, that's in my hall of fame. You've used this before in the seduction stuff, yes?

John: Yes.

Paul: "If you were to…" Write down "Paul's number one favorite."

"If you were to come into the office today" – look at this next one – "I can't be the one to say" – that's a great setup phrase – "when might be the best time for you to do that."

"I can't be the one to say…" Not only is it a setup phrase, but write down "False profession of ignorance."

When you find yourself easily and naturally using the false profession of ignorance, what you're really doing is the false profession of ignorance is taking away any resistance, any thought of "Oh, he's a know-it-all/Well, look at Mr. Smartypants, telling me what I'm going to experience." It's taking away the sense that you're a know-it-all or that you're a pushy salesperson.

"I can't be the one to say when"—"when" is a presupposition of time—"might be the best time for you to do that. I can do X, Y, or Z. If you were to pick one, which do you think works best."

So he used this, and he started to increase his onboarding by 25% or 30%, which, as you can imagine, made a giant difference in his business.

John: Wow.

Paul: As we're going through these tools together, you have to be the one to find the leverage points. I don't know your business sufficiently well to tell you which tools are going to bring you the most leverage. I do know that that paragraph that we came up for you is going to be a great one.

John: Got it.

Paul: I'm very happy with this. I've taught myself something. I think that paragraph alone was worth the whole thing.

Chapter 13
Subtle Words for Super-Agents

Author's note: This bonus section is a transcript of an interview I did on a hugely popular podcast "Super-Agents Live."

The interviewer did a fabulous job firing me up with some very good questions, and as you follow along, I think you'll find yourself growing even more clear in your understanding of my teachings and just what they can do for you.

Enjoy.

Toby: Welcome to Super Agents Live. This is the one place where you can come and hear the most successful people in real estate. You'll hear how these Super Agents built their businesses, how they stay productive, and how they stay motivated. Who am I? My name is Toby Salgado and I made my first million in real estate. I'm your host for the next 30 minutes while we talk to yet another amazing real estate entrepreneur. Stay tuned.

What's up? Hey, hey, hey, hey. Today, this is the first podcast of 2017. I'm excited to do it. Now, today's episode is a very special episode. Look, I get emails all the time. "Hey, can you bring me on your show?" I get agents saying, "Hey, my client, would you consider having him on the show?" I'll look at the bios. Sometimes I say yes, sometimes I say no, but a lot of times I'll go, "Sure, yeah. Put something on tape, and if it's good, I'll release it."

Now this guy, I had no idea who he was. This guy is a massive, massive, massive superstar. Every now and again on this show, I feel like we come up with some magic. I feel like we uncover something that is just like wow, and today's episode, for me, I felt that way.

This guy is a persuasion expert and throughout this conversation, he shares with me and you how to... You have to listen to this whole thing all the way through and you probably want to listen to this one twice.

I've heard everybody. I've never heard a human being explain these persuasion techniques in this way. Overall, he shows us how to use language and phrasing to build trust and to give people positive feelings.

We get into this thing super quick, and the first thing he says is "I'm going to show you how to insert embedded commands in your language," and he goes on to share how we use commands and suggestions in our normal conversations just by using certain phrasing.

I did this one six weeks ago maybe, and I knew it was a special one. I believed in my bones it was a special one, so I wanted to be careful about release, and I have to tell you even before I uploaded into the software today, I was like "Is this the right time? Is this the right time?" I don't know. Guys, I almost feel poorer because this episode is not in my library. It's not in my catalog. I'm not holding this piece of gold back ready to unleash it at any time. I really, really hope you enjoy it. I hope you enjoy it as much as I did.

Hey, let's get to it. Real quick: SuperAgentsLive.com, the show notes will be there. You can follow me on Twitter @SuperAgentsLive. But look, let's just get to it. Guys, if you get something out of this, I want you to do two things. Send the guest an email and thank him for it and send me an email and share with me something you got out of it.

All right, let's get to it.

Today on the show, we're doing something a little bit different. Today's guest is a master hypnotist, transformational healer, change worker. This guy has been on radio, TV, print interviews. He's done everything. I'm thrilled to welcome Paul Ross.

Paul: Thank you. It's my honor and pleasure to be addressing your audience.

Toby: Listen, just so we can tune everybody in here. You have a very rich background, Paul. Really, what we're going to try to get to… Because I know you're a big speaker, I know you're a big trainer. All the stuff that you've learned along the way, our audience can apply it to sales persuasion. That's where we're going to get. We're going to bounce around here, which is what we normally do.

Paul, tell me a little bit about who you are. Who are you, man?

Paul: Well, let me get very quick and make a long story very short. Up until 1987—and I'm 58 years old now—I was the guy who could not get a girlfriend to save his life. I was the best friend, the buddy, the brother, but couldn't get anywhere, and I was determined to solve that problem. As a result, I have into studying neuro-linguistic programming, which is basically, as I would define it, the science of how language structures people's thinking and from there, their decision-making and from their decision-making, their actions.

There's a big model in neuro-linguistic programming that looks at how to use hypnosis in a conversational way. Now if you're freaked out about the word "hypnosis," just think of it in terms of unconscious influence.

What people need to recognize is that it's the unconscious that makes the decisions. So if you can learn to use your language to first capture and lead your prospect's imagination and emotions, you can create a filter to which they view you, a filter of trust, a filter of fascination, a filter of wanting to decide the way you want them to decide.

And my outrageous claim—and it's a bold claim, it's an audacious claim—is if you know how to use language, within five to ten minutes in that initial discussion, you can structure it so that people look at you through that window of feeling connected to you, feeling trusting, and then throughout the rest of the conversion, whenever objections come up, you can reframe those objections so that they actually become reasons for the prospect to buy from you, to list with you, etc.

That's what I'd like to discuss today.

Toby: I think everybody would like to discuss that. Ultimately, I would love for you to give me an example of that because I hear what you're saying, and I know what NLP is, but I can't necessarily… Unconscious influence. Can you give me a…?

Paul: Yes, absolutely. There are different prospects. There are different points in the sales process. If someone comes to you, for example, and they want to list a home… I'm assuming we're speaking to real estate agents, correct?

Toby: Yes, absolutely. Ninety percent of who's listening right now.

Paul: Someone comes to you, or you come to them, and they're interested in listing their home with you, there are all sorts of possible obstacles that you face. "Well, we already have someone," or "Why should we go with you?" or "Let us think it over," etc.

My claim is that what you want to do right away is when you first make that introduction—and this is going to sound a little bit odd, a little bit out there, a little bit strange—is to use something called embedded commands.

Embedded commands work like this. Let's say that you want the person to link to you their desire to sell the home. This is going to sound crazy, but you'd say something along the lines of "You know, as you stop and think about the process of getting your home listed and sold for exactly the price or even more than you're looking for, I'm not sure exactly how you'll find it. I can be the person who does that for you, but as that's taking place why don't we have a brief conversation about what it is you're looking for in an agent?"

Now, that little bit of patter that sounds so much like a mouthful is actually giving many embedded commands. Let me define what an embedded command is.

Toby: Yes, please.

Paul: If I walk right up to a prospect and I say, "I'm the best choice for you as an agent or realtor, you will focus on me and you will pick me above everything else," what do you think that person would do?

Toby: I don't know.

Paul: They'd kick you out.

Toby: Yes, completely dismiss you.

Paul: Completely dismiss you.

But instead… And this is something that the father of modern hypnotherapy, Milton Erickson, specialized in. He built a method so that you could put commands and suggestions in what sounds like an ordinary normal conversation.

For example, if I wanted someone to think about what they really want in a realtor or an agent, I wouldn't give them that command directly. I'd say, "You know, before we get going today, as you stop and think about what it is you really want in an agent." What is that going to cause them to do? That's going to cause them to dip into their imagination and think about it. I'm not sure exactly what comes to mind.

And then what you do—and this sounds crazy—is you would do an anchor. An anchor means a little bit of gesture where you very slightly point to yourself and you say, "But as that's taking place, I just want to let you know it's my honor to be here to serve you."

Now, this sounds like a huge amount of patter, but what are you doing here with this patter? What you're doing is you're setting up in their mind that they're going to go into their imagination. They're going to imagine exactly what they want in an agent. They're going to link that to you, even though you don't specifically know what it is they're looking for. Then the entire process that you go through them, they're going to link that connection and trust to you.

What essentially you're doing is you're creating a filter of trust, of fascination, of wanting to be led, and you're putting that filter between you and them so that they look at the entire transaction through that.

Here's the problem that most sales people have.

Toby: Hold on. I want to stop you, Paul. Sorry, buddy. this is fascinating, man. In your example, "I want you to stop…." In the way that you even deliver that "I want you to stop…"—and you paused—"…and I want you to imagine…" I get that. Now, just one second ago, you said you're going to put these people into a position of them wanting to be led. Because you certainly took command... "Paul, I want you to stop, think about what you want in a podcast host."

Paul: Actually, what I said was subtlety different. I said, "If you were to stop…"

Toby: Ah, okay.

Paul: I didn't say "I want you to," because they'll say, "Want? I don't care what you want." I used something I call a setup phrase, and a setup phrase is something like "if you were to…" or "if it should happen that you…"

What a setup phrase does—and I have an odd technical terminology—is it sets a person up so the commands slide in. I didn't say "I want you to stop." I said "If you were to stop and imagine exactly what it is exactly what it is you're looking for in an agent, I'm not sure exactly what that is or how you put that together as we speak today, but as that's taking place, what I want you to know it's really my pleasure and my honor to be able to be of service to you."

Now, that sounds ridiculous.

Toby: No, it doesn't at all. Let me ask some questions here, Paul. I know that you do a lot of these but is there a downside? I speak that way. I would say, "I want you to stop." "Hey, Paul. I want you to stop for a second." I say that, but is there a downside to me saying that, or should I reframe that?

Paul: Well, here's the issue. If you were to say, "I want you to stop," a lot of people, that would get their hackles up. And could it work if you do it congruently and strongly enough with a certain type of personality? Yes, it would, but I don't want to take the risk.

One of the principles I say is whatever you can get a person to imagine for themselves will be perceived by them as being their own thought, and one of the best ways to do that is to be vague.

So when I say, "If you were to stop and imagine just what it is you want in an agent," I'm not specific. I'm not saying "If you would stop and think about the fact that you want an agent who's reliable, who'll be there for you." That may not be what they want. I want them to fill in the blank for themselves.

What this way of speaking does is it creates a blank in their mind. They have to dip down into the unconscious—that's the real decision-maker—and very quickly come up with their own reasons that they will then automatically apply to you. So it seems to them that you actually fit that, even though you may not fit it at all.

Toby: Right. So you said earlier, these are embedded commands, and you said something along the lines, Paul, earlier up, that you're putting them in a state of mind—again, you said something like this—that they want to be led.

Now, in terms of leading people and you're framing yourself as the leader, you're framing yourself as the person taking control, I would imagine that just like regular hypnosis, some people are much more open to that than others.

Somebody like me, I'm a straight hard-driving entrepreneur, I would imagine that this process won't work as well on me as some person who is a mid-level manager at somewhere else.

Paul: Okay. Let me redefine what I mean by "led." I don't mean that I'm going to be the boss and tell you what you should or shouldn't do. I'm simply creating the perception in your mind that I'm someone who you should follow.

Now, consciously if I said that, you would resist, but inside of every human being, no matter how consciously or habitually they may be as an adult walking through an adult world, inside of every human being is that more childlike part that wants to be led, that wants to be convinced.

What we're doing—and you have to decide for yourself the ethics of it—is in a sense bypassing the adult personality and dipping into that much more unconscious level that people operated on.

You have to understand that 90% of our decisions are made unconsciously anyway. The unconscious essentially has the maturity and the level of sophistication of a three- to five-year-old child.

Essentially, I wouldn't be butting heads with you, and yes, you're a hard-charging guy, and I understand, But the way I phrase things, you're still going to fill things in with your own imagination.

And I never said directly "I want you to let me lead you." If I were to say that directly, you'd kick me where the sun don't shine. What I'm doing is using suggestion to create the perception in your mind that "Oh, I am a leader. You should follow."

I never said in that chain of commands "I want you to let me lead you." I would never say that. Rather, I'm giving the perception that I'm a leader because you're imagining for yourself what you want in an agent, and I'm covertly linking it to me. But your point is a valid one and well taken.

Toby: Again, this is turning out to be a super interesting situation for me, Paul. When you are getting into and reaching that person's subconscious mind or unconscious mind and the maturity level is three to five, that's our reptilian brain where we're looking for danger and – you said something similar. No?

Paul: With all due respect, no. That's just the childlike part of our mind. The reptilian brain is something that goes way deeper than that, and that's not something that can be reached with trance or hypnotic work.

Toby: Okay. I appreciate that. My question or my thought to you, Paul, is if it's not your reptilian brain but it's our three- to five-year-old self, some people are more prone to fear and some others are really confident. If you are tapping into this, could you potentially tap into something that would work against you? You're talking to this three- to five-year-old person and they're rooted in fear, and then you can't get them off…

Paul: That's exactly correct. What we call this in NLP is inoculation, and I'll unpack that bit of technical jargon. In the physical world, if you don't want to get a disease, you inoculate first before the disease takes place. And whatever you think of vaccines—put that controversy aside—you get a vaccine, for example, against smallpox. So should it arise the problem is already handled. So what we're doing in offering the right chain of suggestions is we're inoculating against that fear response. We're making sure that that fear response does not come up.

Let me put it to you this way. A person will not perceive that you're an authority or an expert on where they should go unless they've perceived that you're an authority or an expert on where they're already at.

Now, if you're specific and try to describe to them where they're already at, you may get it wrong factually. But when you cause them to go inside their imagination and imagine for themselves that you're already the person who understands them, even though you may not know any of the specifics, then that averts away from the response of fear. It will create that trust.

Here's a key axiom I will offer to your audience. If you get this, you could increase your closings and conversions by 30% or more just by this one principle. The principle is this: a good persuader, a good salesperson knows when to be vague and call upon the imagination and when to be specific.

Being specific means you explain the structure of the deal, what the numbers are, what the offer is. That's all well and good, but before you do that, you want to capture the unconscious mind and link authority and trust and that childlike desire to believe and be led to you. Then when you present the facts and data it's more likely to go through the part of the mind that's not so skeptical and so critical.

Now, you have to evaluate for yourself whether the tools are fair to use. Absolutely they can be misused; I'm assuming that it's for a win-win outcome here. That's the biggest distinction between persuasion and manipulation. So I hope that answers your question.

Toby: Yes. We're getting there. I have a lot of questions here.

Paul: Ask away.

Toby: I'm going to. Let me just talk in real life for me. On top of this podcast, we have an ad agency and I put people on radio and television. Now, when somebody comes to me and they go, "Hey, Toby. I'm interested in radio," I have this pitch, but it's really education. I tell them what we do.

Now, buying that kind of media is very, very challenging and there's a lot of moving pieces. So I go through, I talk to them about demographics, and I talk to them about cost per point and all this stuff, and by the time I get done with that, they're so confused by it—and I'm not meaning to confuse them—that they just go, "I give in, let's go."

Paul: "I give in" meaning "I want to sign up" or "Let me think about it"?

Toby: They give in to the fact, like "Okay. If I'm going to do radio, you're my guy. I know that I'm not qualified on my own to do this, so I want you to lead me." That's what I mean by "I give up," like "I got it." I can do all this in one phone call. I exude authority.

With NLP, can we do this sort of thing in one setting, or does it have to stack on top of one another?

Paul: Yes. What I want to say is your method is good; I think you'd improve your method if you first said something very vague in the beginning to pace the fact that they're going to be confused.

If they're going to be confused, if you know for a fact that's going to be a response, then what you have to do is bring it up and tell them the conclusion they should reach from being confused.

Some people will think the meaning of being confused is "I need to think about it more." Since you know they may be confused, you want to pace that and lead them to the conclusion that being confused absolutely means that you're the expert and they want to go with you.

I'm sure some people may not reach that conclusion. The response may be "This is overwhelming,"—whether they tell you that or not—"let me think about it."

Toby: Yes. They do tell me that.

Paul: Let me just say this. I wasn't planning on bringing this up because it is an advanced technique that I teach in my training, but I will on the podcast since you brought it up.

Toby: Thanks.

Paul: Knowing when to artfully confuse people can be a very, very powerful tool in your persuasion toolkit. Confusing people without deliberateness or doing it accidentally is not good, but a little confusion, in the beginning, can be useful.

When I give a talk, I'll start by saying, "Some of the things I'm going to present to you today will seem like what you already know. You'll think, 'Okay, I already know that.' Some of what I'm going to present may seem a little bit out there but not too much of a stretch. You'll say, 'Okay. I'm going to try that.'

"The majority of what I'm going to present is going to seem so far out there, so off the wall, at first, you might think this is crazy. There's where I want to challenge you. I want to challenge you to get curious when that takes place because it's the very ideas that stand so far outside of what you're used to thinking and doing that have the best possibility of bringing you the results greater than you're used to having and enjoying."

So what have I done there? I've thought "What are the three possible responses people can have to me? What's the one that I'd better really, really handle? That response of thinking it's nuts and crazy. I'm telling them "When that comes up, here's the way you should respond to it."

So tying this back to your point... And you really have me on the spot here, so I'm just rolling this off the tip of my tongue and the top of my head. If you were to say, "As we're going along today and I'm explaining this to you, there's a lot here and should at any point, you experience any confusion, that's only a sign that reaching for clarity by asking the right questions in an easy thing to do."

What you can do is take that confusion and let them know, "Oh, I'm feeling confused. That must mean that he's the authority and I should trust him more."

The idea is if you know a response that someone's going to have, what you want to do is inoculate against it by bringing it up and suggesting what it's going to mean to them when that takes place.

For example, if you have an offer on the table, someone may experience a little hesitation; they're not sure. That's just natural; it's a big ticket, big money item. So what you might want to do is say, "As you're reviewing this, I'm not sure exactly which part you'll find really, really attractive to you that you want to take action, but as that's taking place, I just want to let you know please feel free to ask any questions to allow you to know you're going to make a great decision today."

What does that do? It means any time they ask questions, it doesn't mean they're skeptical; it just means, "Oh, I'm asking these questions because I do want to make the decision and I want his help in clarifying."

What you're doing is converting skepticism and mistrust as the reasons why they're asking the questions into "Oh. I want to buy. I'm asking these question not because I'm cynical; I'm asking these questions because I need some more clarification."

You can actually change the unconscious meaning people give to bringing up objections and questions. Instead of their thinking, "Oh, my objection means I don't want to do this," unconsciously their interpretation is "Oh, it's not even really an objection. I want to do this. I trust this person. I just need some clarity."

Now, what would it mean to you if you could do that in your business; if you could take people who object or ask questions because they're cynical and don't trust you and turn the very meaning of asking those questions or making those objections, that the meaning the person attaches to that is "Oh. I do really want to go forward with the deal"? What would that do for your bottom line and your numbers? I think it would do it great.

Toby: I would do a ton of good. We don't need to go all day and talk about this, but buying this type of media is expensive. Radio and television can be very expensive. And before I onboard anybody, I need to know that they completely trust me 100%.

Here's what I do, for better or for worse, I do my thing. I build a little relationship with them, and if I sense any kind of hesitation on them or that they don't completely trust me, you know what I do? I just say, "Go away. I'm not your guy. Go do it on your own."

Paul: You're losing a lot of business that way.

Toby: I'm losing a lot of revenue. You know what? Here's what I hope. I'll tell you, my hope is they go, "Oh, crap. I can't do it. I need to change my attitude as a prospect." I'm hoping that they'll come back with a different viewpoint, a different attitude.

Many times, when I'll do this by email, I commonly get an email back from them going, "Listen, Toby. Look. No offense. I didn't at all mean to say that I don't think your system or model works. It's just this or this or this." Many times, like a jerk that I can be, I don't even answer those questions. I'm like "Okay, I'll wait until they get back in line and then I'll onboard them."

But, Paul, do you know how many times that happens? Like 10%. So I have 90% of the people walking out the door and the people that I sell this stuff to, there's not a whole lot of them who can spend three, five, ten thousand dollars a month.

Paul: Right. Of course not.

Toby: Let me ask you this. You're going to help tune me up, and I have no doubt that you can just from the 29 minutes we spent on the phone. But when we communicate with people, Paul, and you know this—you have better numbers than I do—30% is verbal but 70% is our body language. We communicate more with how we hold ourself and position ourself. How does that body language impact our verbal…?

Paul: Let me address this, because a lot of what you just said is commonly accepted; but inside of that, a lot of it is just not true. I want you to think about this critically. In what unit of measurement do you measure responsiveness? There's no unit of measurement. It's not like inches. How can you say percentage of communication? Communication is not measured in any kind of measurable scientific unit, like grams, pounds, etc.

Toby: That's true.

Paul: So when they quantify things like that and say 70% is nonverbal, well 70% specifically is measured by what? I get the general point. If you take it as a metaphor that 70%… Here's the distinction I'd make. There's digital and there's analog. Digital are the actual words you say and then analog are the things that vary along a range. I'll give you a metaphor. There are some lights that you either flick them on or off. There are some lights that have a dimmer switch; you can go from dim all the way to bright.

Analogs are things that vary a longer range like voice tempo, voice volume, voice tonality, voice intonation. Those are analogs. Digital are the words you specifically say. I would say it's 50/50, not 70/30. As a general metaphor, it's 50/50. The specific words you say are extremely important if you want to be hypnotic, but then again, so is your tonality, so is your posture.

I don't agree that it's 70/30 at all. In my experience, it's more like 50/50, and a whole lot of that has to do with how you use your voice, as opposed to how you hold yourself or how you stand. I know that counterintuitive and goes against conventional wisdom, but it's been my direct experience and direct experience of thousands of my students that that's how it works.

Now, there's one exception. The one exception is if you're a public speaker. If you're a public speaker, there is a certain body language that you have to convey. And I do train public speaking as well, but if you're not doing public speaking, I really don't think it's quite as important. There are some books that you can get that are much better than I could possibly teach. It's not something that I'm an expert in.

Toby: I would buy that to a point, for sure. So if I'm speaking with you, and let's assume that you give me a little coaching and can speak in the way that you speak and I get to a point or around a point that I want you to say yes to, I want you to agree to, and I'm explaining it to you and my head is bouncing up and down, I'm nodding while I'm telling you this…

Paul: You don't want to do that.

Toby: You don't?

Paul: No. That's too obvious. It's like the yes ladder. People are used to it. They've seen it. This is another reason why I'm proud of my work, because what used to work no longer does.

Toby: Interesting.

Paul: They're more sophisticated. They know it. They know the tagline questions. They know the yes ladders. They know the head nods. They know "Oh, comment on the trophy on the wall; get them to talk about their personal interests."

Number one, we're living in the age of Twitter and Tinder, if you're into that, and Facebook and instant messaging. People don't have time to pay attention to that. They're ADD and scattered in focus. More importantly, they've seen it before. They're sophisticated. It doesn't work.

I talk about what I call the subtle head nod. The subtle head nod is a very, very small movement of the head that's only picked up unconsciously. If I see them do that very subtle head nod back, then I know I've have them or at least I'm on the path to it.

I teach this. It's the unconscious subtle head nod, because here's the thing. Here's another principle I want people to get. The unconscious mind is not influenced by big, giant movements. It's influenced by micromovements and little small things, because that's the job of the unconscious mind. The job of the unconscious mind is to pick up those small things and small signals that the conscious mind is just too dumb or preoccupied with to notice.

You always want to make your movements small. People are going to look at you like "What? Is he a bobble toy?" No. Counterintuitively what I say is do what I call the subtle head nod. Make everything subtle. Subtlety nod your head, make your gestures subtle. Subtle is significant. Subtle is powerful.

Toby: Help me understand this, Paul. Again, I can get that, I can buy it, but how does that tie into the fact that when we're talking and we're reaching people and using our embedded commands… The unconscious mind, you said, is the three- to five-year-old self. At the unconscious level, is that three- to five-year-old person sophisticated enough to pick up and sense those micro-movements?

Paul: Yes, absolutely. Think about it. When a child is three, four, or five years old, that child has to understand what's going on around him or her in the world and their verbal capability is quite limited, so they have to be able to pick up on unconscious cues. They have to know when their parents are accepting, when they're angry, "Is the environment dangerous, is it safe to go forward, is it safe to explore, should I go backwards?" So yes, absolutely.

This is the reason why magicians will tell you they don't want to work in front of young kids, because young kids cannot be misdirected. The kids catch them. Adults are easily fooled. Talk to any magician. My nephew is a magician. I'm bragging. He has his own 700-seat theater in Maui dedicated to his shows. He'll tell you, really young children, five or younger, they're just too good at catching things.

Toby: That's interesting.

Paul: Does that address your question?

Toby: It absolutely does. Absolutely. Let me ask you this, I went to UCSD. I graduated with a degree in sociology and religious studies. Those were my two degrees.

Paul: Oh, wow. Cool.

Toby: Now one of the things I loved in sociology is this kind of stuff, like how to influence people, because I've always been a sales guy. There's an experiment... I'll try to say this really briefly; you might be aware of it. There was an experiment when we used to have phone booths. These researchers, when you could use a dime to make a phone call, they left a dime in the phone booth. They walked out, and then waited until somebody came in and came out.

I don't know how many people they asked but they asked this question. "Oh, I'm sorry. I was just in there. I think I left my dime in there. Did you see it?" or something to that effect. Now, one group they just asked it to and 80% of those people said, "No. I didn't see a dime in there." Now, the other group they asked that same question but they touched them, even imperceptibility touched them, and some crazy high number like 90% said, "Oh, yeah. I did see your dime. Here is it." How can you use those sorts of things in conjunction...?

Paul: Yes. I get your question. That's making my point for me, first of all. It was a very subtle touch. It wasn't like clap them on the shoulder, I'm willing to believe. Because subtle things like a subtle touch, not like... You know they teach you give them that firm handshake and wrap your hand around their wrist and that sort of thing. I'm not sure about that.

Toby: No. I hate that.

Paul: I wouldn't do that. No, everyone hates it. Everyone knows that it's such a gimmick – please. Like I said, the old stuff just doesn't work the way it used to.

I would say yes, use it. And something I do teach is when to do very subtle touches, very light touches. Some people don't like to be touched at all. Something you need to do is what we call an NLP calibrate. You need to test the individual very covertly and very small to see how their response is to something.

My answer would be combine the verbal techniques with not just a subtle touch but also what I call the self-point...

Toby: Hold on, wait. Paul, I want to hear that but before you do that I want to say one of the things I think we're going to get off this touching bit. I was at a conference a year ago, and this guy I had met before, I wanted to meet him again. We had a conversation, and it was a good conversation.

There was three of us there and we all enjoyed it. I was leaving and when he... This is on the handshake. When he put his hand out to shake my hand, most people will put their hand out and their palm is pointing to the straight left, like a car door.

Paul: Correct.

Toby: Now, what this guy did to me... And this is proving your point because I registered it. It stopped me for a second and then I registered it afterwards. He literally put his hand flat as if he was giving me something and he spread out his fingers, and he was saying "Hey, shake my hand." He was like offering me something and for a second I was like, "What?" I shook his hand, and I just knew there was something unique about what just happened there.

I said good-bye, walked away, and I figured it out. I'm like, "He was like offering me something." Ever since then, I've shook everybody's hand exactly like that. It was a feeling. It was a connection. It was weird.

Paul: Right. And it was a subtle thing.

Toby: It was subtle.

Paul: Subtle is significant. That ties back to the point of the difference in using embedded commands and embedded suggestions versus directly telling someone what response you want them to have. Subtle works. Subtle is powerful. Subtle has power.

Toby: I love it.

Paul: Subtle is significant.

Toby: The finger point. How do you use that? I think that's what you were just getting into.

Paul: Very, very simply. I can tell you what it isn't first because it's hard to describe a behavior over a podcast since people can't see me. But I'll tell you what it's not. It's not like you're calling in an airstrike and vigorously pointing to yourself. It would just be you put your hand to your chest and very small micro-movement, tap your chest. Very, very small movement.

Another way to do this is if you have a piece of jewelry, just tap on the piece of jewelry, that sort of thing. It's what we call setting a physical anchor. Again, it's such a small movement that consciously it's not picked up on.

This is something tying back to the beginning of the conversation. Milton Erickson was the hypnotist at Bandler and Grinder, the founders of NLP studied, in. Erickson was a master at doing these subtle nonverbal things to activate the unconscious mind of his patients. He learned of art of physical subtlety. So you want to keep everything so subtle that the conscious mind doesn't pick it up.

Generally speaking, if the movement is really large, people either catch and/or it will activate the parasympathetic nervous system. That's the part of the nervous system that's responsible for fight or flight, which you don't want to do. That's the neurobiology of it. It's the science behind it.

Toby: When I tap my chest or tap my jewelry, as you said, in a very subtle way, what exactly am I anchoring? The fact that I'm the guy?

Paul: You're anchoring the suggestions that you're giving. If I say to someone, "When you stop and think about it is you really want in an agent. I'm not sure what that is, but as you continue to imagine that," and would just subtlety tap myself, "I'm happy that I'm here to be of service to you." I'd do that subtle head nod.

Toby: Got it. All right. So larger movements will activate your parasympathetic fight-or-flight system.

Paul: Right. I learned this through insomnia cure. I used to suffer from two and a half years of insomnia, and I tried all sorts of things. Then I picked up something where they said just make the smallest little movements in your finger. When you breathe in, lift the finger, and when you exhale, let it drop. But make the movement so small that someone would have to be an inch away to see them.

When you make those small little movements, it turns off the mind that's constantly turning and the parasympathetic system, which is responsible for fight or flight. Excuse me, it's the other way around. I apologize. The sympathetic nervous system is responsible for fight or flight. The parasympathetic is designed to calm you down.

Those small movements turn on the parasympathetic nervous system, which is designed to calm you down. That's the neurobiology of it. That's the science behind it.

Toby: Okay. Large movements will activate the sympathetic flight-or-fight.

Paul: Correct. Correct.

Toby: Now, we've established the tonality and rhythm, the way we use our voice, is important. With my voice, I'm sure you can tell, if you met me in the real world, I can be loud and I'm very much a big movement guy. If you saw what I was doing right now and all the way through this, that's just how I move. That's how I talk.

My voice, being big and shifting from ups and downs, could that in on itself activate somebody's sympathetic fight-or-flight...?

Paul: No. In fact, being able to modulate your voice, which is what is you do, is what we call prosody. Prosody in voice is what makes people's voice melodious and it makes people want to listen to them. For example, monotone. If I spoke like this to you throughout the whole interview and said "When you give suggestions..." no one wants to hear it.

But you know, one of the things I do is I know how to pause in a way that creates that response potential, so people want to hear what I say carefully.

Now, did you notice what I did in there? At the end of it, I put in a command: "Hear what I say carefully." So I created curiosity and response potential by pacing my voice in a certain way, so you were sort of mentally leaning forward, and then I slid in the suggestion "Listen carefully." All these tools tie in and work together.

There's nothing wrong with your voice. You have a great voice. One thing I would suggest to you is learning the art of when to slow down, when you really want to create a little more response potential. That's part of the training that I'll give you.

Toby: I'll tell you, that is a huge negative in the way I talk because my brain works way faster than my mouth and sometimes I'm trying to get something out and I will literally stutter.

Paul: Yes, we can work with that, too. We can slow you down with that, too.

Toby: I want to ask you something because I thought I heard something and maybe I didn't. Maybe I imagined it, but when you were saying "I want you to listen to what I say," you paused very carefully. I thought I heard you snap. Did you snap? Did you give me an anchor?

Paul: No. In fact, what I'm doing is I'm playing with a thumb drive here, which I shouldn't be doing during an interview.

Toby: Okay. All right. This is absolutely fascinating. We have to wrap up. Let me just ask you a couple of quick rapid-fire questions before we let you go, Paul.

Paul: Sure.

Toby: We covered a lot of ground. What's something I didn't ask you that I should have asked you? What's some one really important thing that we just didn't…?

Paul: This is a whole other training but I would say what is the best way to go about establishing a realistic motivation and an informed enthusiasm? We know sales can be very up and down. If you depend on your feelings of the moment or the events of the day you can't create a vision that pulls you toward your goals. How do you do that?

I did an entire mind frame training on this, this afternoon. My quick answer is take on a learning frame, and the learning frame is "I'm interested in the sale. I'm invested in my skills." The distinction between interested and invested is this. In a breakfast of bacon and eggs, the chicken is interested; the pig is invested. I hope you get my metaphor.

Toby: Got it. Yes, totally. Okay.

Now the one question before we wrap up for good, Paul, is this. Do you have a daily habit that you think has contributed to your success?

Paul: Yes. I meditate.

Toby: This is the deal, Paul. I always encourage my audience. If they've have anything out of this, reach out to you and say thank you. Where can people find more about you? Where can people connect with you?

Paul: Here's what to do. If you're interested in having me speak to your organization or at your event, or train your team, just go to SpeakerPaulRoss.com to find out how you can do so now.

Toby:. Hey, Paul. I will kick off the thank-you train. Thank you, man. I know that you're busy. I know you're always on the TV, radio. Everybody wants a slice of your attention, so I appreciate you taking the time out and sharing with me and my audience.

Paul: It's my honor and pleasure. You've been a great host.

Toby: Thank you, man. Talk to you soon.

Paul: Bye now.

Postscript

We've come a long way together since this journey began, and I have to congratulate you on your moment to moment decision to keep learning, keep practicing, and most of all, keep taking action.

After all, I'm sure you will agree that is the action takers in this world that reach their dreams, and even beyond.

It's my sincere hope that this book has shown you the potential of using your language in a concise, directed and powerful way.

While some of the concepts may have shaken you up, I hope they have equally and even more powerfully opened your eyes to new ways of doing things.

Remember: it is the very ways of thinking, feeling and acting that stand so far outside of what you have been used to doing that bear the potential to bring rewards and results that are so far beyond what you have been used to enjoying.

Thank you for the privilege of being your teacher, mentor and guide and should you find yourself thinking, "I'd like to hire Paul to speak at my event/train my organization/ teach my team" you can get that ball rolling by going to SpeakerPaulRoss.com.

Paul Ross
Feb 2019
San Diego California

PS: If you have success stories from using the concepts and tools in this book, please email me at: success@SpeakerPaulRoss.com.

Book Paul Ross
as your next great Speaker, Trainer, or Teacher.

Ross is available for:

- Keynotes
- Breakout presentations
- Speaking to groups and organizations
- Training of large or small teams
- Seminars and teaching

To contact Paul's team for inquires/booking, go to SpeakerPaulRoss.com.

Made in the USA
Coppell, TX
20 August 2021